T0128134

Whimsy and Spice

Whimsy and Spice

NOT EVERYTHING NICE

ISAAC M. FLORES

WHIMSY AND SPICE
NOT EVERYTHING NICE

iUniverse books may be ordered through booksellers or by contacting:

iUniverse
1663 Liberty Drive
Bloomington, IN 47403
www.iuniverse.com
1-800-Authors (1-800-288-4677)

ISBN: 978-1-4917-6212-7 (sc)
ISBN: 978-1-4917-6211-0 (e)

Library of Congress Control Number: 2015903752

Print information available on the last page.

iUniverse rev. date: 04/14/2015

Dedication Page

This book is dedicated to the fond
memory of my late wife,

Dorothy Anne

Contents

Short Stories

Calendar Love

We bow to the future
and sigh for the past.
We love and remember

and dream to the last.

But for all the bold lies
that the almanacs hold,
while there is love in our hearts

we can never grow old.

(In tribute to my friend Perry E. Gresham)

Hello World

"Hello, world. Are you ready for me?"
My tiny granddaugher shouts out those words
through the screen door, standing there
sillhoutted against the bright dawning sky
of a warm winter day.

She is almost 2 and still in her polka-dotted
pajamas, just out of bed, short hair thick and rumpled.

Ay, Ay, it's easy for me now to re-live those perfect
times when the world was young
and so were she and I.

"See, grandpa," she says as she turns and comes
running to my open arms, seeking my approval.
Her beseeching dark eyes
opening even wider.

I applaud, of course, and we sit at the kitchen
table, eating our cereal and waiting for the rest
of them to come trekking in one by one.

We are anxious, we two, to get started
to begin another perfect day in that perfect
world of long ago,

gone forever if not for
my daytime dreams.

So Sad

It's oh so sad
when all the songs
my heart yearns to sing

have been sung,

when all the words my soul feels
some others have spun.

It's oh so sad.

I long to tell of my love
I crave to shout it in song,
but all must remain unsaid,

because . . .

all the words have been written
all the songs have been sung.

Why?

There are many things that I set out to do and never do.
I mean some honest-to-gosh good things
that I wished I'd done and never did.
I write long detailed notes telling myself what to do
and when
but I don't.
Don't ask me

Why?

Like, I've meant to change the carpet, for 15 years,
and repaint the house
and wipe out the that pesky hornets' nest with my whiz-
bang spray gun
(One flit and, whoosh they're gone).
But no, I haven't done those things.

Why?

Like writing a poem about my orange-ish cactus
flowers,
Or making up the lyrics to a tune I've just composed,
Or contacting a friend I haven't seen in years.
But, no, I haven't done those things either.

Why?

Why didn't I call and say I still love you
After all these years.
Maybe you would have come back to me
Or me to you. But, no, and please don't ask me

Why?

Gracie

Black and fat,
Gracie the Cat.

Wrongly named, for graceful you are not
in crazy race with imagined roach or rat.
Bounding, scratching,
common — one could say —
lest you sidle and with pleading eye
roll and beg: rub my belly, pat and play.

Idle time away,
Gracie seems to say,
I defy you to ignore me.

If you manage, anyway, Gracie shrugs
and slinks away,
disdainful, seeming, but ever with a sway.

A wary eye, forever searching,
then furtively leaping, fur a-flying.

Is mother close at hand
for feeding, stroking and a lap for lying?

Ah, Gracie,
you give us cause to contemplate
our own mysterious fates.
We ponder, in wonder, your strangely quiet pauses
like inward clauses,
with furry pawses hiding green-brown eyes.

We know a soul you have
and a power to recall
a friendly step, a favorite food,
a special smell, a petting hand.

Intelligent eyes that see the world dewily,
Is that a smile, half sardonic-ly?
Refusing to be ignored.

Thus, in a hasty world all around,
we stop to do your bidding,
rewarding a persistence seemingly unbound.

Pinch of Salt

You know your friends are getting old
when minor events of yesteryear
become grand acts
of heroism past, in the telling.

So a warning to us all: When some old geezer
starts spinning tales of wondrous bygone days,
listen attentively, politely,

but sprinkle lightly with several grains of salt
and ensure a full shaker is always at the ready.
for it goes from fact to fiction in a flash.
They "fib and tailor for posterity," as writer
Timothy Egan puts it.

Be that as it may,
some people, young or old,
who listen carefully
seem never to forget.

They appropriate your real adventures
and soon start cracking
your own sweet tales
back to you,
as their own episodes of derring-do,
that far surpass what once was true.

American Beauty

She was a stopper.
a real American beauty
when she was young and full of life.

Oval face framed with dark hair
sometimes long and flowing,
often short in flapper style
with curled bang on pale forehead.

Creamy skin, trim figure, well-fitted
in simple dresses with printed, yellow flowers
and white, pleated collars worn low.

Accompanied now, in this sepia-brown and faded photo
by an equally young, light-suited man with middle-
parted hair.

My mother- and father-to-be so long ago,
smiling, with not a clue as to what lay ahead
when their Great Depression would bring
a dead end stop to any dreams of future bliss.

Ozymandias

Who was Ozymandias?

King of Kings, you say:
Ramses, from a lengthy line of royalty,
but which, and who was who?

Who, in truth, was Ozymandias?
Was he King of Kings, on his tomb inscribed?

Given second life by Shelley's verse,
which resulted from a traveler who said,
"On the sand a shattered visage lies,
A wrinkled lip and sneer of cold command . . ."

Yet, little trace remains
of that unrecorded time and place.
"Look on my work, ye Mighty, and despair."
That, too, inscribed in history's trace.

Where he reigned, 'tis said,
was in a misbegotten desert land
in ancient Egyptian sand.

Who was Ozymandias of mythology
Was he Ramses, and if so
was it I, II, III or just phraseology?

Did he a kingdom rule?
And what did the poet really know
merely talking to the traveler in London-fair?

Some say a philosopher he.
But Ozymandia's nature lives
only to the curious such as we.

Poet Billy

Billy Collins creates
A treasury of simple heartfelt truths,
the vivid scenery of everyday life,
seemingly ho-hum but ever so new.

It seems to me he always has a stew.

Billy Collins jokingly argues
there are just too many poets around.
But the trouble with *The Trouble With Poetry* is
that it *encourages* more of us to write — poetry.

It's said that Billy Collins is too easily read.
Perhaps.

The truth, however:
Many a reader will pass through,
going along with the cozy words and rhythms,
giving little thought to the profound,
revealing truths that lie beneath.

It once was said, I forget by who,
"He writes of the undramatic,
the non-momentous,
the etcetera of life."

John Updike once wrote of a
"saint of the mundane,"
which I don't think quite applies
to my friend Billy.

And yet . . .

Perhaps our once, or is it twice-
Poet Laureate of these United States
would permit a version,
just a taste, of his particular
brand of spice, so nice:

Young girls pray these days
not only in churches or by bedsides,
but just about wherever they go.
In shopping malls, in school and play,

Oh My God! they do exclaim
with an awe that seems to me
an endless, brainless but oh so-cool refrain.

First Love

The scent of lipstick,
Your body leaning toward mine.
As we walked, I talked.

That long, searching look
that came to your eyes
like a curious cloud, a searching question,
never asked, never answered.

And, later, the radiance of your smile
made any hurtful things worthwhile.

Such contentment is all that remains
as I lie in my bed at dawn's sweet glow.

Someone wisely said,
Such a great love never comes twice.
Once it's gone, it won't come back.
This you learn,
regretting, but never forgetting.

Starlight

You and I were young once.
Your eyes shining bright,
your lovely face, so cool to touch,
your hair dark as raven's wing,

in starlight.

Another age, you say.
Yes, but once again to treasure now,

in starlight.

We loved, then grew apart.
Now we are here,
faces close on your pillow,
tearful eyes gleaming,

in starlight.

Then, too soon,
you closed those eyes
to mine, forever,
never again for me to see,

in starlight.

Always There

I know you are there
when I laugh with my friends
or wallow in sorrow.

I know you are there
when I wake and I sigh
on a long summer night.

I know you're still there
when shades silently creep
causing curtains to stir
with no breeze in the air.

I just know you are there
for death cannot still
the true love we share.

Certified

A friendly, more learned fellow than I could ever be
Once philosophized about life to me, so huskily:

"Ya gets a birth certificate when you're born,
and some poor soul gets your death certificate when
you die.

Seems to me, the guv'mint could provide
something in-between —
a handy way to prove that you're existin'
and leadin' the kind of life you're able,

With all the good times and the bad,
whatever God's put on the table,
the lovin' and the terrors
and the cruelties that forgettin' we've been able."

Forgetful

Old men forget.
And maybe we, ourselves,
will soon be forgotten.

But, in our late years, we see ourselves as
having been kind, orderly, successful.
It seems we forget our many misdeeds
in our up-and-down lives.

And, most of all,
maybe I've said this,
perhaps we forget
our great regrets.

British barrister-novelist John Mortimer
(creator of the abiding character Rumpole of the Old
Bailey)
once wrote, "Being young is a time for growing used to
disappointment."

Most of us wouldn't admit to that,
now, would we?

Dream

You've come back into my dream.
You are back to lie beside me.
To sit with me,
to talk to me

and chide me.

But you won't say
why you went away.
And I don't care
so long as you can stay

beside me.

If you leave again,
I'll thrash around
and, finally sleep. with hopes to dream
of a coming night

when you will lie beside me.

Crepusculo Twice

Here are two beautiful words I have known
throughout these many years and only vaguely
knew their meanings,
crepusculo in Spanish and *crepuscular* in English.

In my gathering years, I've learned that crepuscular
is an adjective meant to convey that special time of day
called twilight.

It carries that same meaning as an adjective in Spanish.

The Spanish noun crepusculo is a word whose meaning
is defined by me as that short and brilliant interval
before sunset, when the mountains and desert flowers
are silhouetted as unforgettable images on the far
horizon
of my brain.

There is also a morning crepusculo during which
soaring peaks and desert cacti
appear purple against the orange and yellow colors
of another beautiful sunny day
in my native Southwest.

Grandpa

Oh how I reveled in that child's cry,
Grandpa!

I waited impatiently for workday to end
when, greeting, she would shout,
Grandpa!

I'd lived long and hard
and believed little else would move me
until she would run into eager arms
and with a loving sigh would whisper,
Grandpa.

Oh how that simple memory stirs me still,
Grandpa.

A Life Too Short

He lived to be thirteen,
Too short a life to make,
they said.

Better to die young, innocent, happy,
they said.

The pain and sorrow of a mother, father, brother
would one day disappear,
they said.

The mind regrets, accepts, forgets,
they said.

Somehow, that day is yet to come
and is not soon expected.

No one can comprehend
unless he and she are destined to remain behind.

Then, a young son's death
is never ending, never forgotten.

The End

I can no longer pretend,
I can no longer deny the pain,
I give up, I give in.

Please understand
and forgive, if you can.

You know I know pain,
what you may not
is that it's never left.

This ever-increasing affliction
is now overcoming
not just body, but mind and reason.

And, finally,
after all that transpires,
I can no longer resist.

So, I pray,
in the end
you will know

why I abruptly departed.

Could've, Should've

Along about now, you're maybe thinking,
"I could have written that." And you're probably right.

And,
You could probably cook a cheese omelette
avec l'oignon et petit pois just like that French chef
on TV.

Or,
you could maybe redo your basement
as good as that master craftman in the illustrated book.

And,
keep a lush, green lawn better'n that expert
on the "Saturday Garden Show."

Or,
write corny poems such as these,
something simple, like that.

Who knows . . .

But why wait?
Come on, come on,
join me in the world of make-believe.

This is what writer Enid Bagnold had to say
about who wants to become a writer. And why?

"Because it's the answer to everything. ...
It's the streaming reason for living.
To note, to pin down, to build up, to create,
to be astonished at nothing, to cherish the oddities,
to let nothing go down the drain, to make something,
to make a great flower out of life, even if it's only a
cactus."

America's Peril

The great Czech writer Milan Kundera once said,
"A nation which loses awareness of its past gradually
loses its self."
Isn't that what's happening to us now?

There are few out there who could tell you
why the American Civil War took place and when,
where the Gettysburg Address was delivered or by
whom,
What the Reconstruction Period accomplished,
who James Madison was and some of his achievements.

What about FDR and his New Deal,
Truman and his comment, "The Buck Stops Here,"
and the atomic bomb?
LBJ and Civil Rights?
When and why did the Great Depression take place?
Why did our country decide to send men to the moon?
Remember Grant and Lee? Woodrow Wilson? the
Wright Brothers?
Alexander Graham Bell and Henry Ford?

Bedrocks of the building blocks of "enduring
democracy,"
that has now evolved into a grandly modern society
in which everything is taken for granted,
where law hardly exists.

as if slavery were not legally abolished,
as if independence and free expression came to us
overnight.
as if the poor are there because that's just the way
things are.
Right?

"Only at your own peril can you be indifferent to the
past,"
Kundera and other thinkers argue.
Our society accelerates its downward droop
if we continue to fail
to apply those hard-learned lessons
of the past to our present and our future.

Crazy World

This world is going to hell in a hurry
And, you will have to forgive me,

When I say I'm glad to be leaving here
Before it gets there so completely.

Leaving Soon

I sit and wait and watch,
as the world filters past.

I don't know what I wait for,
nor do I much care.

But I see what's going on,
even though the years have
strained my brain.

What I see, I mostly don't like,
but don't mind me.
Pay it no never-mind.

I sometimes watch the TV set,
or read old friends such as D.H.
or e.e. and dear ol' Billy C.

But, in plain truth,
I won't miss the world I see,
maybe not even the internet.

It's not such a sad thing for me to say
that I'll be going soon to see
if there might somewhere be
a bit more pleasant view.

Life or Death

People sometimes ask
whether I believe in an
afterlife.

In other words, what do I think of death —
is it a new beginning or the end, period.

I tell them I know everything
I want to know about death,

and that is that it's inevitable
and that's all I wish to know.

We all must wait and see,
until such time it comes upon us.

Would an afterlife be
bettter, worse or in-between?

I have too many challenges to overcome
right here and now to worry
about some murky, unforeseen.

Though callous it may seem,
my waiting time spills over

with day-to-day renascence
of the man I used to be.

History

The amazing thing to me
is the history we don't know.

Harry Truman's words
echo back to us
in this embattled world.

Too often, we choose to forget
and that may be a greater crime,
and one we've come to regret.

Sleeping or Waking

A friend once said to me,
I seem to do my best writing at night.
I tried it too.

Alas, my body seeks the bed
while my brain is taking time in waking
from its hibernation
of the night before

Foolhardy Poet

When I get the swell head
and start to think I'm grand,
I reach to my shelf and open to
Shakespeare, Sandburg,
D.H. Lawrence and such.

I then marvel and sigh.
Mere words and scribbles won't do,
says I,
shaking my head and putting down pen,
returning the next day to start this anew.

And when I do, it's obvious for sure,
to make a simple poem come true,
One needs
deeper thought, greater emotion,
and "character," too.

and certain *élan*.

A poet sees a deeper soul, a stormier sea,
a happier heart, a more desperate love and
a flower-ier desert

than me.

Still, I stay. What else to do?
After an hour or three,
I look at my paper and what do I get?

A headache, a heartache and more stomach acidity.

Who?

Who makes you laugh and sigh?
Who makes you fuss
and sometimes cry?

To whom have you whispered
"I will love you 'til I die?"

But now you go,
Without a why
And me to wonder, who.

And why there was
No sad goodbye.

Ditty

(As 5- and 6-year-olds we sang this nonsense out of the hearing of our schoolteacher nuns, who patrolled the classrooms like Hitler's henchmen)

Hickory, dickory, dock,
The monkey ran up the tree.
Hickory, dickory, dock,

sha-la, sha-la, sha-la.

Hickory, dickory, dock,
Poor monkey's lost in the tree.
sha-la, sha-la.

By now, it's plain to see,
that losted monkey
in a tall banana tree

is just really little ol' me,
sha-la, sha-la, sha-la.

What to do, what to do,
woe is me, to be or not to be
in a school not meant for you or me,

sha-la, sha-la, sha-la.

For Truly Sure

Know you this,
for truly sure,
my deserts and my mountains.

I will always be your lover
though you may forever
sit so lonely . . .
and so nobly all endure.

Lover's Lament

How can you be
but you are not?

How can it be that you are here
and say you love me
when it seems you're far away
and deep within yourself?

I can see you and feel you
and go through the motions

and then everlastingly suffer
when you seem not to care
just . . . as if you're not there.

Where? Where can you be
when you truly are not here.

Ode to a Teacher

Miss Lucy Cobb,
I so shyly adored you then
and so often recall you now.

Miss Cobb, you taught me well,
that everything is possible
if you believe you can.

You and sister Mary,
teachers both
and spinsters, too.

You knew me well,
before I knew myself.

How fully you knew
a boy who grew
strong and proud
because of you.

Random Thought

We on this planet are like a half-blackened lonely leaf
somehow finding itself floating aimlessly
amidst a vast dark sea,

journeying fast and furious with little-known trajectory,
helpless in a sea of hazards, never knowing what fate
awaits.

Or, as John Steinbeck once wrote, "Like a jellyfish
washing up on an inhospitable shore."

No, too many won't agree.
There must be purpose there,
or are some things just meant to be?

Dorothy

Dorothy Anne's ashes lie lonely
in a pleasant graveyard beneath a marble plaque
engraved with name, birthdate and the day of death,

tended to with flowers fresh or silk.

Pine trees swirl in the wind
flags flutter their colors
and a sculpture of the Lord looks
down on everything below.

Visits diminish as years fly past,
old age afflicts some who are left behind.

All is peace and quiet
as in the end she prayed for.
But then I grieved. My love was gone.
My love, Dorothy, took it with her.

Confess

It troubled me then, and it bothers me still.
To think that you can commit a grievous sin,
confess to a man in a box behind a screen,

who imposes your pennance — maybe
three *Pater Nosters* and five *Hail Marys*
and a quarter in the box for a candle.

and, bang, after "contrition" you receive "absolution,"
Perhaps never again to pay serious mind
to the commandments you've broken,
the crimes you've committed

or the people you've harmed.

Your slate wiped clean, ready to restart
on that evil road you've taken
and the life you seem to have forsaken.

Until the next time you need absolution.

On Writing

I wish I could write the way I would like it to be,
flowing soft and easy, or tough and aggressive
whatever it calls out to be.

Under limited circumstances, I do the best I can.
My only defense is I write about life
as I live it.

Life is a school of philosophy.

Somerset Maughan once too-modestly said
about his prolific output,
"It was the best I could hope for . . .
with the very limited powers
granted to me by nature."

George Orwell had this to say
about his profession,

"Writing a book is a horrible, exhausting struggle,
like a long bout of some painful illness.
One would never undertake such a thing
if one were not driven on by some demon
whom one can neither resist nor understand."

And Philip Roth,
"The road to hell is paved with works-in-progress."

After all that, who would want to do all that . . .
but all of us fools who try.

A Long Day

The day isn't long enough
for me.

During one day, alone,
I mutter about my many chores,
I read, write, argue with myself

aloud.

I replace three boards on a fence,
I write,
read the entire daily newspaper,
and think, I make notes
and walk and talk

to me.

I visit a friend and Google around
I drive to the grocer, and chat and buy
my next dinner
and replenish my cookie supply.

Tben, a bit sudden, darkness appears,
the day almost done.
much too soon, it seems

to me.

I eat, drink a Beck's and watch a little TV
then slowly prepare for bed,
reread some Whitman, Sandburg or Collins
and maybe, if I'm lucky,

finish a poem of my own,
and falteringly start in on another.

Finally, with great displeasure,
I drag to bed — and continue to think,
lying there sleepless.

until I finally conclude,
I'm weary.
So I end a short but quite a productive day,

for me.

Fancy Place

She takes a bite of food and calls to busy waiter.
"I asked for medium-cooked steak, please,"
pushing a plate of bloody meat gently towards him.

"Be right back," says he, whisking it away.
We sip and wait, nipping at our salads.

A tall, authoritative gent quite soon appears
and showily places a fresh dish with another steak and
garnish.
She smiles and says to suave manager standing there,
waiting for approval,

"It looks just right, but I'd like some A-1 steak sauce,
please."
Our man looks horrified and blurts out,
"Oh, no ma'm. We don't carry any of those.

"You see, our kitchen knows its business."

We shrug and smile, drink and smile,
eat our steaks,
and shake with all-out laughter, too.

That's all that's left to do
as we pay the check and go skidoo.

Such is Life

Sometimes the more you know
the more you wish you didn't know,
my aging friend keeps on a'sayin'.

I know too many trivial things about me
dealing with the medical,
he says, while sitting and a'rocking and a'sippin'
some bitter-lookin' gray-black tea.

As a for instance, he continues,
I've about used up all the synovial fluid there was,
causing joints and bones and ligaments to collide
and pain me dreadfully.

This so-called Arthur-itis is moved 'genetically'
through the ol' family tree, my doc confides in me.

More'n three feet of large intestine was once taken
by what that ol' doc called a transverse resectional
caused by the Big-C in my middle,
the ol' man shrugs and sips.

Another noted surgeon cleaned up this
crooked ol' spine and replaced a few vertabry.
A metal plate
with screws and such was implanted deep within.

The name of that procedure
is somewhere
else recorded for posterity.

But never mind, I get along,
my pal sums up.
I pray this righteous life continue,
painful though it often be, says he.

Killing Brain Cells

A dear friend always intoned, before savoring his drink,
"Well, let's kill some more brain cells, my friend."

I remember the last time,
Just before we went to war.

We were dining at a favorite shrimp-and-steak place on
the beach.
And, while waiting for our table, we sat drinking
and killing brain cells in the cool, tree-shaded patio,
marveling at the setting sun.

"Well, let's kill some more,"
says he, hoisting a second Margarita.
"Salud," I nod solemnly sipping.

After another, we move inside as the sun escapes the
horizon.
and ate our steak dinner with some aged pinot noir.
Then he packed up and left, and I never saw him again.

To this day, I remember
the last time we had drinks and a steak,
just before he went off to war and was slain.
Now, he may still be in France, one of those icognito American
G.I.s buried under well-tended green sod,
with yellow flowers often trampled by laughing
schoolgirls passing by.

I am near ninety,
But plenty of brain cells remain
for me to miss him immensely.

For, if he were here, we'd be hoisting a few,
killing more brain cells
and joyously recalling the fun days.
And the sadness of saying *adieu*.

Pancho Villa

He rose from serfdom to banditry,
And when labeled a hero by the common man
became a highly respected general
in the puzzling and deadly Mexican Revolution.

From that sound beginning, a stubborn streak
and independent ways of defending the landless peasant
soon labeled him a criminal under the law.

Because of American involvement,
He led a small nondescript unit into
a whirlwind invasion of U.S. territory
at a windblown border town called Columbus,

terrorizing citizenry, looting rifles, ammo and horses,
all the while exchanging gunfire with American army
troops and townfolk.

His escape through the deserts and gulleys of northern
Mexico
once again made him a hero to his own, and a criminal
to the U.S.
He set out then to re-organize an army strong enough
to overthrow now-corrupt governing powers in the
Mexican capital.

But the going got rough, and changing leadership threw
that country and its people once again into a muddle
from which they're still emerging.

Long embattled, Pancho Villa soon retired on his own
terms.
But along his stormy way in life
he had made as many enemies as he did friends . . .

And on a hot July morning in 1923, the old
revolutionary
was at the wheel of his Dodge saloon in a rural town
called Parral
when he and his entourage were gunned down
by a volley of gunfire set up by those enemies.

The news of Pancho's assassination
led to much soul-searching among his countrymen.
Was he considered a patriot or a traitor to his country,
did he more good than evil?
After all, one widely read newspaper, El Universal, of
Mexico City,
wrote,"No one but him has defied our neighbor
and no one has dared to do as much against them as
he has."

Oligarchs and landed gentry did not mourn,
but the inspiration of hacienda peon won the day.

After more than half a century of virtual oblivion,
Pancho Villa's remains were transferred to Mexico City
and there reburied with full military honors
at the Monument to the Revolution.

Thus, ironically, he rests alongside his long-dead
enemies.
Their old bones have sometimes been described
as The Uncomfortable Dead.

Florida Killers

Unasked, and probably unheeded, advice
for you soon-to-be retirees dreaming of Paradise:

Florida is a place where you are more likely to be killed
by a mosquito than those notorious sharks or 'gators.

Check it out.
A disease-carrying mosquito.
Often unseen, seldom heard
until too late.
Usually, but not always, on a humid night.

The mosquito can easily sneak into your room.
sharks and 'gators never, ever do.

Need I tell you of our 'canes?
They hardly ever sneak,
but killers, they be too.

So, for all you neophytes,
I'll keep this short
and tell you what.

don't move to Florida,
whatever else you do.
'Cause now you have a clue or two.

Special Goodbye

Now she's gone they will wonder,
and mutely pray a special goodbye,
each in his own secret way.
They will desperately miss her,
even quietly cry.
And so will I.

Land of Nada

Florida.
'Tis hardly a place,
it is a state of mind.

In days of old,
pathfinding Spaniards
called this paradise
La Florída de Nada.

No silver or gold,
just swamps and trees and lakes and mangroves
with furious mosquitoes and man-eating *lagártos.*
Vamonos — and they left.

Florida is now a destination.

'Though ill-chosen by conquistadores,
a forlorn, sub-tropical peninsula
becomes a busy mecca — for tourists, retirees,
beachgoers and opportunists of all stripe.

Grudgingly, but surely, *La Florída de Nada*
grandly survives all comers
and lives, so famously, forever after.

Perfect World

They were the perfect couple, everybody said.
They lived in their own private perfect world,
their perfect little house set in a perfectly manicured
garden

with pink azaleas and lush-green hanging baskets,

A sliding door leading to a showcase of a greenhouse
with perfectly potted dahlias and purple orchids.

Theirs was a perfect little kitchen set off by wide
and polished windows from which to gaze at the passing
world,
most often upon elegantly dressed ladies
walking white poodles to and fro.

The perfect little library provided burnished wooden
tables
and roomy overstuffed chairs where one could sit
and peruse Shakespeare sonnets at one's will.

And the living room was one of wonder, full of ivory
figurines,
silver salvers and many knick-knacks from afar. Soft
lamplight shone
on silvered sateen walls featuring priceless paintings
done by masters.

One perfect summer evening as the sun was slowly settling,
Two gunshots pierced the stirring breezes as if coming from within that glorious house.

Neighbors and a curious passerby found the perfect couple
lying in the hallway,
lifeless bodies side by side,
their blood-red gore already drying
on the perfect parquet floor,

A pistol with its gleaming burnished barrel lying near their perfect bedroom door.

Book Critique

Listen here, everybody.
You gotta go out and buy a book.
That's right, a book.
You gotta go out and buy a book written by Walter E.
Mosley.

A book featuring a black man-about-town,
a most-moral crimestopper by the name of Easy
Rawlins,
A Red Death.
is the book's name.

Fabulous.

W.E.M. is just plain good —
black or white. Nobody's really better.
You'll see.

But you gotta go out and buy the book.
Don't wait around for a movie. It might not happen,
with all the stuff that's in this book.
A Red Death.

Coming Soon

If the self-labeled Islamic State
doesn't get its own way,
If Israel and Hamas don't destroy themselves
and us before then,
If Vladimir Putin does not continue
to expand Russia's borders,

then, this planet will destroy
its very own self.
And soon.
All we have to do to cause this great event
is nothing.

Let's continue to ignore
our environment.
Inexorably and inevitably,
nature will take its course.
Our planet will disappear.
Many small fragments will take our place
in the cosmos.

"Ah," some onlooker in space
will in some distant future say,
"What were those stupid people thinking?"

I Say

I say I don't believe in God, and
that there is (or was) a Supreme Being
who exists there, somewhere, in 'Heaven,'
beyond the cosmos, I would guess.

That He created everything, everything
on this earth, and maybe others, too.

How could that be, I say.
I believe in the evolution of all species,
as demonstrated quite well by Darwin

and the legions of scientists in fields
and white lab coats,
and by deep-thinking philosophers
and writers of explicatory notes.

I believe, I say, that creation
of the creatures on this earth
and everything around them
evolved over hundreds of millions of years ago
and were certainly not created about, um,
6,000 years ago or so.

Then, why is it, I say,
I often find myself
looking up beyond the clouds

and fervently saying, Praise the Lord
and Thank You God.

Civil Wrongs

How can you claim rights
when you're out breaking windows
and burning stores
to steal beer and whiskey?
How can you claim rights
when you are committing wrongs
in the name of the dead?

Lonely Leaf

We on this planet are like a half-blackened lonely leaf
that somehow finds itself in the middle of a vast ocean,

journeying fast and furious with little-known trajectory.
helpless in a sea of hazards, never knowing what fate
awaits.

Or, . . . as John Steinbeck once said,
"Like a jellyfish washed up on an inhospitable shore."

Fidelity

A good friend once said to me
explaining his fidelity,
Ugly she may be, but
who better understands poor me?

Said she to me, quietly,
he's good when he wants,
and he wants what I want
when we want it.

He's happy with it,
and she seems to be.
So they stay, and happily succeed
In a good and simple life,

this understanding man and
his plain and saintly wife.

In-Between

A friendly, more learned fellow than I could ever be
Once philosophized about life to me, so huskily:

"Ya gets a birth certificate when you're born,
and some poor soul gets your death certificate when
you die.

Seems to me, the guv'mint could provide
something in-between —

a handy way to prove that you're now existin'
and leadin' the kind of life you're able
with all the good times and the bad,
whatever God's put on the table,
the lovin' and the terrors
and the cruelties that forgetin' we've been able."

The Woodsman

His muscles gleam with sweat
His sinuous neck and arms strain.
His day stretches from the earth's first light
until the wonder-filled dark surrounds him and
slowly releases him to rest and ponder.

After,
he sleeps the tranquility of a day's work done
of good life lived.
He wakes to the prattling of birds, the rustle of leaves
that drop as silently as the dawn's first flush.
His coming day is like the others.
He immerses body and soul into the daily labor
as if he knows no other.

His massive shoulders will not again feel
the caress of a softly starched shirt.
His feet will not embrace the
supple leather made for ballrooms.
His love has gone.

He is alone
and may never know another world.
But he is here, he is full, he is home.

Just Another Day

There was high sky this winterish day.
Little wind. no tree branches
waving frantically at their neighbors.
Few leaves scuddering on the ground.
Fluffy clouds rarely bothering the sun.

It was a sort of day that wouldn't declare itself,
sunny, but cold in shade.
Oh, well, he muttered. it just can't decide.

It was a day like today
that reminded him of boyhood

when he walked in desert sage,
weaving his way among cacti,
heading for snowy mountainside,
lazily hunting cottontail for supper.

But he was old today and limped.
Happy to be free to roam,
away from dusty rooms
and forever-squawking bird in cage.

Not many steps away, an ambulance hurried by,
its red lights warning, clear the way.

Walking on, friends came up to say,
that was Francis who has gone.
It just looks as if his time has come.
Done. And left us here and waiting.

One small consolation left,
the old man said, and knew
friend Frank could but agree.

He thought it rather foolish,
but said it anyway,

Frank would not have chosen
a more glorious winterish day.

Independence Moon

Slowly, slowly lifting — timidly poking
through far west horizon
it snoops over the golden rim
where land first meets the sky.

A faint glimmer through eucalyptus branches,
spawning ghostly reflections on blackened lakewater,
this moon is shy and hesitates,
seeming lost and wandering.

Suddenly, it seems God has lost control
of these abruptly blossoming skies . . .
Dark night is brightening now!

Ablaze with glowing, manmade, multicolored 'works'
booming for this special night.

Deep reds, hazy-lazy multi-hues
and spidery white webs
conglomerate when once
there was merely flickering light.

It is our nation's independence we now celebrate.
And now, here too, is that rounding orb,
overcoming modesty, submitting
its own silent, growing tribute.

Our own Independence Moon.

It could have been ignored, at first its light so slight.
But, as if gently urged by cosmos gods, it blooms,
elegant, serene and robust
until its hazy pumpkin beauty is unmatched
by those reds, whites and blues lighting up our humid
summer sky.

Now it radiates, this ever-lovelier sphere
aggressively shouldering its way
onto our shifting gaze while we marvel
and strain to see its every move.

But, too soon, the stormy clouds appear
and again enclose the night in dark.
Our moon then fades and rockets cease to glare.

My eyes mist, or is it rain,
as we slowly walk to where we came.

And, so it is,
that until the morning sun fails
to light this fading brain,
that mystic Independence Moon
will be by me remembered as a
lovely *arco iris.*

a joyful burst of freedom,
on a glorious Independence night.

Book on a Shelf

Hey, look me over
please don't pass me by.
Oh me, O my

how I would cry,

if you were to scorn
and skip along and say,
It will wait another day

and then quickly walk away.

Perhaps to save the day
your friend would smile
and glance my way
and shyly say,

Bye, Bye.

Mystery

I find myself sometimes getting up
from my easy chair after an hour or so
of reading.

And saying out loud to no one,
"Where am I? . . . Who am I."

And later as I walk to my kitchen,
I can hear myself muttering
as I pour a second beer,

"*Why* am I . . ."
which seems more *apropos*.

But I'll never know,
Why, indeed?

Musical Distraction

And, yet, we all know that
everything is all right
in this world where there
in front of your eyes, on
Public Television,
is Lawrence Welk. distorting
another piece of American music.

But, no, I get some criticism
for just saying that.
Some say he demolishes European
music equally well.

And, don't forget,
Canadian and Mexican
and Cuban . . .
They say Asian, too,
and even Minnesotan!

Short Stories

Short Stories

*Over the course of many years, stories build
up and then decide to spill over.
Eventually they find themselves written
down, as you see them now.*

The Soul Saver

He was my special friend and comforter. I suspect he knew. But I never told him so, much to my regret.

He was the shoe repairman in town. I was 8 and then 10 and then 12 and 15.

"John —The Sole Saver," said the elegantly printed sign on his shop window. But John was more than that to our little town. The *soul* saver probably would have been a more apt slogan on his sign.

My friend and his little repair shop, which fronted on a streetcorner in this two-stoplight town, played a crucial part in the economy of our community. I can see that now. He was making sure his customers' shoes were always wearable. That was a significant part of everyday life, strange as it may seem today.

The cobbler's shop was a wonder to me as a little boy with big eyes. I had often accompanied my mother or grandmother to "the shoe man."

He was always there, pounding away behind the counter. The repair place was a thriving business. John seemed to know every customer by name and liked to chat about their families and the doings of the day. He seemed to know more about the world outside his little shop than we did.

This was during the Great Depression. In those dark days of the 1930s and early '40s, rich or poor, your shoes told what kind of person you were. They say your shoes are the first thing people notice about you. Well, John must have taken that to heart. And good shoes were like good friends: prized and polished. (Since then, I always make sure about that).

Clean clothes and shiny shoes — men in well-worn suits, ties and hats, ladies in neat dresses and chapeaus, plus well-kept footwear — made them feel equal to any prosperous executive walking down the street or a banker sitting in his office.

A good appearance gave a person an air of confidence, although things might not have been that way at all.

Well-kept shoes were vitally important, I can see now. Even the out-of-work men in breadlines or out looking for jobs wore their suits and Fedoras and their good shoes. Women wore their flowery dresses and special shoes anytime they went out of the house, even to the Safeway Supermarket.

Most of us walked everywhere we went in that town, and growing kids needed to keep their shoes passably good for school. Hardly anyone wore "tennies" except the well-to-do kids who could afford to buy them in a sporting goods store.

My friend, the cobbler, was maybe in his mid-60s. He was stocky and short, with muscular arms. He had big, brown friendly eyes and usually a smile that I thought for a time was reserved for me, but it turned out to be for everyone stepping into his crowded space, especially for the housewives who often delivered their family's shoes in brown paper bags.

There was a solid wall of shoes behind him in his small shop. Shoes he had resoled, reheeled, rebuilt, some of them many times over. The shoes were in cubbyholes built into a blue wooden shelf along the wall. They held cardboard stubs he would give out when somone brought the shoes in.

He worked right in front of a glass counter, in which he displayed new shoes or those that someone had failed to pick up after years of sitting in a cubby. Some of the shoes were two-toned, black or brown and white, several high heels, some expensive, I guessed.

The shoemaker was kind to me — a thin and gangly, pimple-faced boy who sold his newspapers and shined shoes on that very corner when he was in grade school. John the Sole Saver always looked up and smiled when I shyly walked in for company, reaching up to quiet the tiny bell that tinkled every time someone walked in.

I would often stop in to see him and talk. He encouraged that. As a kid selling papers and even while in high school.

"Ah, Manny, I was thinking you don't come by so often now, you're so busy," he remarked one day when I was in high school.

I assured him I would get better about that.

"I have basketball practice and play a lot of baseball now, too, John," I would try to explain.

We always had long talks while he worked. Widening his eyes, he would tell me about his young days, his "wild days," he called them, in several countries in faraway Europe. He had led an "adventurous life" until he married and came first to New York and then to Chicago and then out West, where he and his wife Lida wound up in this little town, in this little place.

"Sometimes I think I'm as busy as you," I said one day. "But Friday afternoons are good for me."

"Yes, Fridays I stay late," he would say. "But then I can put up the sign — 'CLOSED WEEKENDs' — and then go home, have a glass of wine or two, listen to my wife and read. What better than weekend, no?" (When he had a lot of orders to fill, he would spend half a day at the shop on Saturdays, too, banging away with his hammer and nails until late-afternoon.)

His stories about his adventures and his family, about his early childhood in Poland, his two brothers, both now dead, and his wife, who was devoted to him. greatly appealed to me. He was "worldly," in my view. Lida loved their life in America and had a good meal ready when he got home from a sweaty day's work.

At his urging, I talked about myself, too: about school and family, how everyone worked hard to get by. He would take the time to listen, and to ask a judicious question now and then while he continued to work. He made a kid like me feel comfortable, sharing stories, sometimes laughing at something one or the other said.

The townspeople kept him busy during this time.

Millions out of work, poverty throughout the country. So far as I could tell, however, my family had always been poor and all of us — my great-grandmother, my grandmother and my parents and siblings — didn't notice much difference in our daily lives. In one way or another, all of us kept working to bring food to the table and buy our clothes.

Over the years, I've never forgotten my special friend and the lessons I learned there in that little shop. I'm ashamed to say, however, that his real name escapes me. He had finally told me after my many questions over the years, He even spelled it out on one of his coupon cards for me. But, I've lost the card and forgotten John the Sole Saver's real name.

The memories of that little shop and the kindly old man behind the counter have stayed with me over these many years. And it still pains me to think I never told him how special he was to that little kid who has always been within me.

Walt Kelly, Philosopher

One of the best philosophers of the Twentieth Century (yes, all 100 years of it) was a *cartoonist,* Walt Kelly.

If you haven't done so, read his words and enjoy his drawings and blurbs about the diverse activities of the denizens of the Okefenokee Swamp (especially during a political season — any political season). Many of us forget, or may not know, that he had masses of avid followers of those cartoons and other entertainments during the 1950s and '60s. All without any of the devices of the digital age to spread his output.

Kelly was at his special best before, during and after Congressional and Presidential campaigns of those times. His humorous works, though, have an enduring quality, and one can apply the same attitudes and slithery activities to today's politicians, and probably tomorrow's.

Noisy scandals, obscene conduct in high places, graft, corruption, mudslinging, you name it. They were all there, and these nasty doings seem to go on forever. Get the money, get the votes!

Kelly unraveled it all simply and logically with his pithy, illuminating observations.

"Too much is enough," he one time said.

A close friend, Bill Vaughan, probably explained Kelly best. "In examining the backside of political reporting, Kelly is more informative than the double-domed investigative reporters — and a whole lot funnier," Vaughan wrote.

One could go on and on about Walt Kelly and never say enough. Review his work in still-available books. And you will greet, or remember, a great mind, an everlasting talent for words and images.

Another timeless example, one that has gone down in history:

Pogo the Possum and his animal friends are sitting on tree stumps in the Okefenokee Swamp, enjoying the evening breeze while the sun slowly sets on the horizon. In his quiet, insightful manner, Pogo rolls his big eyes and ruminates about the state of the world in general and politicians in particular. He suddenly ends this little moment by saying, "We have met the enemy, and he is us."

Has anyone ever said it any better than that!

Governor's Trip

(This is a favorite feature story of my early years as a reporter. Strange but true.)

Governor Leaves Louisiana Mental Hospital For a Crazy-Quilt 'Western Tour'

By Ike Flores
Associated Press Writer

Santa Fe, N.M. (AP) -- Once upon a time, Louisiana's famous Governor Earl K. Long suddenly decided to become a tourist and take a driving tour of Texas, New Mexico and Colorado. So he "escaped" from a mental hospital. He what?

Uncle Earl, as he was known to all, had been committed to the institution by his wife and some of his associates, who claimed he was bipolar. He was in the last year of a third term as chief executive of his state. Earl K. was a brother to the better-known Huey P. Long, who had previously served as governor and later as a U.S. senator.

After Uncle Earl's commital, he went on conducting his business from the mental hospital, with the process reportedly filtered through his spouse and other state officials.

But he got antsy. Never mind all that, the eccentric governor decided one bright morning. The accommodations were fine, but he wanted to see some of the places that lay just west of Louisiana. Why not? He could do what he wanted as governor.

He was tired of running the business of state by telephone from the mental institution at Mandeville, and so he ordered the head of the hospital system fired. Uncle Earl then replaced him with a staunch supporter, who promptly released Long to do as he pleased. In effect, Long sprung himself from the mental facility and headed into the sunset, along with a retinue of friends, in several limos. This was in 1960, when Uncle Earl was 64 years old.

There was an uproar back at the statehouse in Baton Rouge, and in the big city of New Orleans and other places. The rural people, who knew Earl Long best, laughed and joked about it. But he didn't care about any of that.

He wanted to take an auto trip. Go for a fling. Suspend all state business for awhile. He liked women, horses and gambling. (Among his female friends was the notorious stripper Blaze Starr.)

One of the colorful governor's first stops on his epic Westward Journey was Juarez, Mexico, a wild and wooly Mexican border town across from El Paso, Texas, where almost anything went — and usually did. He then visited the racetrack at Ruidoso, in southern New Mexico, where money flowed as easily as it had in Juarez. At this point The Associated Press decided that he was "making news" and assigned a reporter to keep tabs on the traveling party.

Easier said than done.

Ol' Earl (another affectionate name) and his mini-motorcade managed to elude what quickly evolved into a gang of newspeople and photographers who were eager to pick up his trail in Albuquerque. Reportedly, he was to stop there and rest overnight. But his fast-moving Cadillac zipped right on through the Duke City and headed north.

I was working for The AP in Santa Fe at the time, and I was called in on the chase. It was my turn, in my bailiwick. He was headed my way!

I got into my trusty '55 Chevy Bel Air and tried to head 'em off at the pass, you might say. If you were in any way imaginative, you could even see the thin dust clouds as the dark-blue Cadillac and several black limos showed up on the outskirts of Santa Fe on U.S. Highway 84, pursued by several cars of reporters breaking speed limits all the way.

This quickly became the reality.

The whole group, including the newspeople, abruptly stopped, however, and checked into an exclusive area resort. The governor was said to have fallen ill! I caught up and checked into the hotel, too.

Ol' Earl's illness became the puzzling malady of the moment. His aides refused to say why they had stopped at this time. What was wrong. His ticker? He had previously had a heart attack. Mental problems? Speculation ran wild. Here was a guy who had just left a mental institution, governor or not! And nobody was being told anything.

We reporters were on the phones with our offices half the night, trying to make sense out of what was panning out to be a hot story. Finally, after hours of bewilderment, a doctor who had been called in explained that the heat and exertion had just tired the governor out, and that he would make a quick recovery.

He sure did!

After an overnight stay, the traveling party hit the trail again. I was now part of the gang. There were short stops. A peek here and there into Santa Fe museums and painters' studios, plus a brief stopover at an Indian village.

After shaking hands with various Indian elders, Long's auto caravan again set out onto the open road: this time headed for the art colony of Taos.

We intrepid reporters were in hot pursuit, busily scribbling in our notebooks wherever we stopped and when we could elbow our way through a motley retinue of the merely curious. The whole motorcade now was preceded by a New Mexico State Police car with sirens and blinking lights. Talk about getting attention along the road.

At mid-afternoon, the speeding automobiles screeched into the stone-and-gravel parking lot of a high-class touristy restaurant on the outskirts of Taos, and everyone enjoyed a leisurely meal of hot, spicy Tex-Mex food on the terraced patio. After that, we all pushed on into the little Taos plaza, which was teeming with tourists and townfolk.

After a short glimpse, that was enough culture for Uncle Earl. Following his lead we all jumped into our automobiles. And just as the entourage was wending its crowded way onto the road leading to the main highway, Earl spotted an Army-Navy surplus store right on a corner of the tiny plaza.

The governor called a halt — a difficult thing for all the drivers concerned in the narrow streets of downtown Taos, but halt everybody did. And after much jockeying, tire-screeching and cursing, everyone was parked and hightailing it into the surplus store after the giggling, arm-waving squatty figure of Earl Long.

Here, the fun began.

"Sonovagun, sonovagun," Gov. Long kept saying, or words to that effect. He was as excited as a kid at

Christmas. "Look at all this good stuff." His eyes were everywhere.

He tried on Army helmet liners, combat boots, fatigue hats and pants, rubberized shoes, rain ponchos and anything else that was handy. He was at the same time bargaining at full voice with the proprietor, trying to lower what he called outrageous prices on the merchandise. He swept through the store like a small tornado, happily intent on buying a wide variety — and large quantities — of clothing and other items for what he said was his "poor, workin' colored-folk back at my ol' pea patch."

He was in fine fettle, posing for photographers and strutting about, talking, cussing and arguing all the while. He poked in bins, under counters, behind doors and in drawers until he was fully satisfied he had seen and bought everything he liked.

Finally, after about an hour of this, Gov. Long tired, and the group was off again, going at full speed up the treacherous, winding, two-lane roads of northern New Mexico, deterred neither by oncoming traffic, darkness, a rainstorm nor the possibility of winding up at the bottom of a deep canyon.

Those of us who managed to keep up with all of this breathed heavy sighs of relief when the governor's retinue sped through Raton in the middle of the night, on up through Raton Pass and into Colorado. (I never knew what mischief he got into there.) From Colorado, he headed back to deal with wife Blanche, his Bourbon Street pals and the turbulent political atmosphere of Louisiana. He had left us panting in his wake.

Whew!

Gov. Earl K. Long died of a heart attack within a month after taking that trip and shortly after completing his third term in office. Only his doctor knew for sure what was wrong with poor ol' Earl.

RIP, guv.

Fixing the Broken

"If it ain't broke, don't fix it."

That's the old redneck wisdom, and oft-professed axiom. when contesting a piece of proposed legislation in many state legislatures.

They get right up there in front, demanding their say with, "Mr. Speaker, Mr. Speaker, sir." They, the freshmen legislators with their perpetually sunburned noses and bellies bulging out of their new white shirts and black striped pants from Sears.

The comical part to close observers in these forums — Santa Fe, Tallahassee and elsewhere — is that each and everyone of these chunky new guys in their red ties fervently believes he created that phrase for this one special occasion. They don't need to make a speech in opposition or express any reason for negativity. That's it, period.

They honestly don't know that this shopworn exclamation has been used by lawmakers everywhere since time immemorial. Some version of it was probably exploited at legislative assemblies held in Roman times, and maybe even before then.

This phrase may still be ringing in legislative halls for years to come. Not just by sunburned rurals in Sunday-go-to-meetin' clothes. It is employed in one way or another by those of intellect who stubbornly choose to go their own independent ways in modern political circles and rule-making assemblies.

Mark Twain once said, "No man's life, liberty or pursuit of happiness is safe while the legislature is in session."

But . . . there it goes again. "If it ain't broke, don't fix it."

Often times, I say, when it's broke, it's way too late to fix it.

The Drunk

You could almost smell him before you saw him weaving from one side of the alley to the other. You felt like turning around and going back to where you started. But you plowed on, toughing it out until he reeled on by, deeper into the alley.

The Drunk and his disheveled clothing reeked from cheap wine, vomit smears and heaven knows what. The other kids all said he would become violent if you came near him. So, stay away. But, then, we kids got scared easily.

The Drunk was in-and-out of that alley, which was wide enough for a big garbage truck to go through every other day. Maybe The Drunk slept in the alley at night, or tucked away against a fence corner in somebody's back yard. Most families had slapdash board fences back there, with garbage cans either neatly arranged or spilling over on their sides.

Some yards opened to the alley, and there was usually a spillover of kids playing ball from one open back yard to the other.

It was an old neighborhood in a small town founded by a railroad man. Most of the houses and yards were tidy, well-kept. Other poorer ones had tacked-on additions, flat roofs and tumbledown garages. But everything was kept decently clean by the housewives and grandmothers, who often left their kitchens to sweep and clean up after messes made by their children.

The Drunk wandered all over the neighborhood. Some of the folks knew him personally, sometimes leaving food for him. Others tried to ignore him, pretending he wasn't around. We kids gave him a wide berth when we saw him coming. We were all scared of him, not having seen anyone like him before.

The man was obviously in dire straits — if you thought about it.

As a kid with big ears, I had heard my family's talk of efforts made in the past to help The Drunk, as everyone called him. Local officials had once placed him in a special institution. After that failed, they tried one "program" or another. Over and over, it seemed he was on the road to recovery when the cheap Muscatel began calling and taking control of him again.

He would then just disappear, apparently down into the deepest pits imaginable. He would just as suddenly reappear — that dazed and smelly drunk who was shuffling around through the alley now.

He was a survivor, this man. Tough, I guess. He was middle-aged but looked older. He had once had a family but they had long ago disowned him. And so he wandered, filthy, bearded, with his wild blood-shot eyes and hair matted down with debris: A sorry sight.

One bright day, as he stumbled through our alley, a little old woman who lived way down towards the end of the block unlatched her back yard gate and waved him in. He hesitated briefly, then lurched on through. The old woman grabbed his arm and helped him in. The last I saw of them, she was helping him up the two steps into the kitchen door of her neat block home with a flat roof.

I had too many other interesting things to do — play with my new archery set, practice my hook shot at the too-high basket nailed to the roof overhang, for instance. So I never thought much about what I had seen.

Weeks later, however, when I again saw The Drunk, he was not drunk. He was walking straight ahead, and he was clean, his grayish hair slicked back and parted in the middle. He had on a neat dark suit, a starched shirt, shined shoes. A hat, even!

He was walking alongside the tiny woman, who always dressed in black and gray. She had her snow-white hair pulled back and walked steadily, purposefully in her gray shoes with the short heels. I watched them go into the nearby church. Today isn't even Sunday, I thought. It was the middle of the afternoon. I should have been in school, but I was home with a "cold," an excuse that my grandmother had reluctantly agreed to go along with.

I thought hard about what I had just seen. I was dumb and curious, so I brazenly decided to ask the woman, whom I vaguely knew only as Mrs. Martinez, about him. Weeks went by before I had my chance, though. I screwed up my courage, finally, because I hadn't seen The Drunk in all that time. I knocked on her kitchen door.

Evidently since I was the only one who had bothered to ask this somewhat aloof old woman about what was going on, she sat me down that day, fed me some oatmeal cookies and a glass of Orange-Crush and told me about it, part of it, anyway.

Mrs. Martinez said she had seen the Drunk, whose name was Javier, time-and-again in the neighborhood. She worried about him. And one cold night when she had trouble sleeping, she told me, she decided that if she really believed in her God, she would try to help Javier.

How could she do that, besides giving him a meal once in a while? She pondered the matter, at church and elsewhere, and decided to throw caution to the winds.

That must not have been easy for an old widow-woman who had managed her life alone for so many years. She was fearful, but gradually found the strength to help — really help — a man like that, who obviously was a very troubled soul.

She was not naturally a do-gooder. And religion didn't much enter into it, she said. After all, she had received that "enlightenment" all of a sudden during a bitter cold night when she was trying to sleep.

"He was afraid, is all it was," she told me, an eagerly nodding, nosy sixth-grader.

"He was afraid to quit drinking. He was afraid something awful would happen. In his lucid moments, he was afraid to change things because he thought disaster would befall. It took someone to be patient enough to listen and understand."

It was that simple, the elderly woman said: patience and understanding, that's what began to help Javier. She gave him the opportunity to talk about himself and his past life.

She offered him a room in her tiny house, where he was warm. She never asked for anything. The neighbors tut-tutted but she gave them no mind. She gave him a little money for some personal needs, but she never saw him drinking or drunk again. He started cleaning up after himself and began doing some needed work around the woman's small property.

And he started going to church with Mrs. Martinez.

Things seemed to be going well, until the fates stepped in once more.

One fine day, two men in dark suits appeared at Mrs. Martinez' door and asked for Javier Monteverde without identifying themselves. He came in out of the back yard, greeted them cordially and took them into his little room in the back of the house. There, all three spent about fifteen minutes in conversation, and then the two men left without a word to the widow.

Late that night, Mrs. Martinez was awakened by a sudden, strange noise. She thought it came from Javier's bedroom. When she made her way there, he wouldn't open the door to her knock. She waited and listened but heard nothing. She knocked louder and called his name. Silence. She tried the doorknob. It turned and she walked in.

The sight sickened her.

In a short time, three policemen in full uniform knocked loudly on the front door. They were soon followed by an ambulance, whose attendants quickly removed the covered body of Javier from the house and sped away in the dark.

He had strangled himself from a ceiling rafter with a bright-colored tie she had bought for him a week earlier.

Later, the grownups in the neighborhood pieced the story together.

Javier had evidently been the unidentified killer of a nine-year-old boy about three years earlier on a nearby farm.

The nine-year-old was slain by a single blow to the head by a tree branch, killed by Javier when the child came upon him as he was scrounging for food one evening at dusk. The boy had been shocked and afraid when he saw this crazy, smelly drunk in the field. He cried out to his mother, to his daddy, and he started to run.

That's when the boy's young life ended and the aimless, drunken wandering of Javier began.

You could say Javier's life ended then, too.

My Friend, the Doctor

"You could be dead, my friend."

That remark is always said jokingly, and it causes us both to laugh — because I agree with him. But it also sends a shudder and a quick prayer through my mind and body. It registers because it is said by my friend and gastroenterologist. You might say he is transparent in his activities, and certainly honest with his patients.

I'm honest with myself, too.

"Man, when I examined you in that hospital bed before your emergency surgery, things didn't look good," he said. I nodded. I sure didn't feel like dancing a samba.

Just before I was discharged from the place, he had told me, "I'm happy you pulled through, man." This was after ten days of tubes, hoses, yucky soft foods, injections and no sleep. I won't go into more detail.

But, finally, Freedom.

My son Mike was waiting to take me home. I was changing into civilian clothes and suddenly blurted, "Wow, I sure could eat a hamburger."

Mike, always quick with a quip, says, "Yeah, we'll first stop by the drugstore and get your medications, and then we'll see where we can get you a good dose of dignity."

Thanks I sure needed that. I recall laughing all the way down the long hospital hallway to check out. And we were still laughing and joshing when we drove to the pharmacy and then to my favorite café, where I soon disposed of a huge hamburger and a glass of tea. I reluctantly turned down a beer and the side of fries.

That was then, quite a while ago it seems.

In the latest episode to this story, I'm lying on a bed in the clinic for another semi-routine test procedure when my young-looking energetic friend, the doctor, steps in in his white mask and gown, tugging on his gloves.

The nurse was adjusting a warm blanket under my feet. The anesthesiologist was starting his thing on my arm, which would knock me unconscious for an hour. Just before I went bye bye, my friend, the G.I. guy, walks up to the bed tugging at his surgical gloves and asks how I'm doing. "My feet are finally warming up . . ." I groggily start to say.

"What are you complaining about," he interrupts with a smile. "You once told me, you're lucky to be alive." I did say that, I remember. We had agreed on that.

The smile was on my face, I know, and then the light went out in my brain for awhile. The procedure seemed to be over quickly. I was soon awake and anxious for the juice and crackers offered by a nurse.

Test result? Don't have to see him again for two more years. Just lucky, I guess.

Che Guevara

One of the major stories to go virtually unreported during my time as a correspondent in Cuba, by me and every other reporter there, was that of the in-house intrigues leading to the now-legendary guerrilla activities in Africa and Latin America of Ernesto "Che" Guevara.

In overly broad terms, the Argentine-born revolutionary (some say mercenary) was bored after four or five years of trying to implement the ambitious objectives of the Fidel Castro insurrection that overthrew dictator Batista.

In 1959, after Batista fled the country, Fidel Castro, Che and their fellow rebels were it. *They* were in charge. They were now responsible for running the country, for instituting the reforms they had vehemently espoused in highly idealistic terms for years. While Fidel was busy replacing people, nationalizing American businesses, expropriating lands and properties, the short, scruffily bearded Che was entrusted with making contact with the Soviet Union and obtaining economic help from other foreign governments, along his more mundane, everyday tasks.

An intelligent, well-educated man — some say an intellectual — Che was an admirer of China's Mao Tse-tung and had been a follower of the Chinese Communist Party line since his university days in Argentina. This, more than anything, experts have determined, formed his thinking about "people's revolutions" in Africa and the Americas.

To be sure, Che spent several years of hard work trying to centralize Cuban industrial production, believing that industrialization would be the salvation of the country after the revolution. He was often at odds in this with Castro and others who were busy expropriating large land holdings and trying to develop agricultural resources.

From his earliest days in Argentina where he studied medicine, Che was by inclination a contrarian, an ardent revolutionary in the true sense of the word, and a born adventurer. Traveling throughout the Andes — usually on his own, sometimes by motorcyle — the young man had ventured through Chile, Peru, Colombia, Venezuela, into the Central American nations and Mexico. He took his time and experienced first hand the oligarchical, autocratic regimes that often fattened themselves at the expense of the poor in many of those countries.

He honed his pro-communist leanings, sometimes joining local causes and movements seeking the overthrow of dictatorships and the established order.

He met Fidel in 1956 in Mexico City, where Che had landed a job teaching at the National University. That's where they hatched their plan for invading Cuba. Mexican security police soon got wind of their recruiting and training activities, however, and jailed them for about a month for plotting to overthrow the Cuban government from Mexico.

That experience was the genesis of the guerrilla movement which in late 1956 resulted in the Granma expedition into Cuba's Sierra Maestra. Out of a force of less than 100 *guerrilleros*, about a dozen men including Fidel, his brother Raul, and Che survived the bloody, short-lived encounters with the Cuban military after the "invasion" and escaped into the mountains of Southeast Cuba.

Reports of a greater number of surviving rebels are not supported by facts.

From the mountains, the relatively few rebels conducted sporadic guerrilla warfare, slowly inspiring poor farmers, students and the unemployed to join their ranks and participate in forays against the military throughout the countryside. This eventually led to terrorist activities in Cuba's villages and larger cities, causing Batista to flee the country in January 1959.

The Castro-Guevara revolution had succeeded in overthrowing the dictator. Now came the hard part: delivering the goods. And, in this, they soon became even more ruthless than the regime they replaced.

Che, a military hero, was proclaimed a "nationalized Cuban" and immediately set about holding military tribunals, jailing and executing hundreds of civilian and military personnel who were suspected — or had actually been part of the Batista government, especially those who had hunted down university student leaders and pro-communist followers.

Che was then appointed to head an Agrarian Reform Institute. He also began specializing in technical and economic matters. About the time I arrived in Cuba as a correspondent, he was president of the National Bank and, later, became minister of industries. As such, he became Cuba's representative in international conferences in Europe, Latin America and the United Nations.

Fidel, of course, always occupied center stage within Cuba and completely overshadowed every activity, and every personality who had the temerity to veer off into a different pathway There were several popular heroes of the revolution who became victims of Fidel's jealousies and simply disappeared from the stage. Thus, Che increasingly became part of the murky background of post-revolutionary Cuba. Despite his foreign travels, his mentions in the international press and his appearances on American television, he began to be pushed aside in Cuba's hierarchy.

After the CIA-led 1961 Bay of Pigs invasion and the October, 1962, missile crisis involving the Soviet Union, the activities of Che Guevara became largely unknown within Cuba. Historians and some of us reporters later pieced together some of the details.

There were occasional reports in the foreign press of his travels in Africa and Latin America in those days, and his appearances at conferences and giving speeches in foreign lands. In February of 1965, in a speech in Algiers, he was quoted in the European press as outlining some of the mistakes of the Cuban revolution. He was said then to be deeply involved in aiding revolutionary and guerrilla activities in several African countries.

In mid-1965 came the fateful and highly mysterious step: Che "resigned" his Cuban citizenship to return to South America to lead armed struggles there against dictatorial regimes. At least that was what the Cuban government said publicly much after the fact.

He surfaced sporadically in one country or another, organizing and training guerrilla groups, until he was killed in a mountain skirmish in Bolivia in October 1967.

His exploits then became hugely embellished into legend. And, in death, he has acquired a cult hero status that he never would have achieved in a long, active lifetime. In Cuba, Che is posthumously regarded second in importance only to Fidel.

Alas, precious little of his personal revolutionary activities were known outside the small group of Castro insiders at the time. As restricted foreign journalists in Cuba, we were as unaware of those activities as people were on the outside of the country. The average Cuban, of course, knew even less, except for the ever-present rumor mill.

They were as surprised by his death — announced by Fidel Castro — as was the rest of the world.

Those circumstances that weren't known during Guevara's busy life have been increasingly clarified after his death, however: Che Guevara never achieved any of his goals in Latin America, and he is *not* the iconic hero conjured up principally by Fidel Castro — on that very public occasion memorializing his death.

Steinbeck's Beliefs

(A thinking man's tidbits in the John Steinbeck novels)

The sweetest reward one can have in this life is when you can feel you are paying your way as you go along in society. "Man owes something to man. If he ignores the debt, it poisons him."

-0-

(in "Sweet Thursday) Where does his discontent start, he wonders. "The pains came . . . like a stir of uneasiness or the flick of a skipped heartbeat. Whisky lost its sharp delight, and the first long pull of beer from frosty glass was not the joy it had been. He stopped listening in the middle of an extended story. He was not genuinely glad to see a friend . . . What am I thinking? What do I want? Where do I want to go. . ."

-0-

"There was nothing he could not do because there was nothing he wanted to do very much."

-0-

"There are people who will say this account is a lie, but a thing isn't necessarily a lie even if it didn't necessarily happen."

-0-

Drinking wine, a small group of friends sits in a saloon, lamenting the loss of a departed friend, and out of their memories, there emerged "a being scarcely human, a dragon of goodness and an angel of guile. In such a way are gods created."

Santa Fe

A light snowfall overnight became ice by morning. And after several attempts, I decided my car was absolutely determined not to go up a little embankment to the street from its secure parking spot.

At times, in fact, it threatened to slide over the side and into a little adjoining arroyo. Better safe than sorry, I decided, picking up the phone to call my office downtown. I would wait until the sun came out, maybe by noon, the way it seemed. I was staying home for awhile.

I wouldn't be taking up daily duties as correspondent at the state capital in Santa Fe. What lawmaker was faithful enough to attend a boring committee meeting, anyway, I thought in a knowing way. Any excuse would do to give politicians a free day. It turned out I was marooned the whole day, while they could have easily gone back and forth to the capitol from their downtown hotels if they had really wanted to do that.

It wasn't a big snowstorm, mind you. But there was plenty of fluffy snow, and then it got really cold. And it all resulted in an unusual, bitter day. There were a few concerns — crested creeks, power outages, fallen tree branches blocking roads and driveways, that sort of thing. Nothing serious.

But in that era, if your landline phone and-or electric lights went out, or your car wouldn't do what you wanted, that was it. In a heavy storm, which happened infrequently, you generally stayed put. No cell phones then, no communication except with your neighbors.

And, maybe, they had a way to get out and maybe not. Mostly, you just puzzled over what might be going on in the outside world.

I'm not talking about living out in the boonies, in the 1960s.

Our house wasn't far from now-famous Canyon Road, which features adobe side-by-side buildings housing artist studios, chic restaurants, gay bars and the like. From Canyon Road, you could take another narrow two-lane gravel road that led to El Caminito, which eventually brought you to my house on Abeyta Street.

Downtown Santa Fe was only 20 minutes away by car, probably hours by walking over snow and ice. The place near my house where I parked my 1954 Chevy was on a downslope from the street, on the flat side next to the craggy, ancient sinkhole or arroyo. You could yell across it to our good neighbors, the writer-poet Witter Bynner and his wife.

Snow in Santa Fe is usually a delightful change in generally delightful weather. The town of about 40,000 (in those days) was unique in my experience. Santa Fe even today calls itself *The City Different*.

I was there when the "ancient city of the holy faith," a melting pot of three cultures and onetime outpost of European civilization in the New World, celebrated its 350th birthday. Let's see . . . that was in 1960. So that would make it well beyond 400 years old at this writing.

The settlement was founded in 1610 by Spanish explorers coming from Mexico. It became the capital of the vast Spanish territory of New Mexico, and it thus became the oldest capital city in the United States.

Santa Fe claims it is unlike any other place in this country. Admirers are quick to point out her peculiar charms, quick to defend her and to resist any move to change her or let her become just another tourist town. Every street and nook and cranny is steeped in history. The few critics mainly deplore its strict zoning laws, which dictate any new construction among other things.

Its Palace of the Governors, the building erected in 1610 to serve as the seat of government, is the oldest public building in the nation. And the city claims to have this country's oldest church and the oldest house, both still in use. Santa Fe goes to great lengths to protect its quaintness and the foreign flavor in its older sections, born of narrow, winding streets tightly bordered by mud-walled houses, some stuccoed, some not.

During its long history, the town has been under the sovereignty of five governments: Spanish, Indian, Mexican, Confederate and the United States of America.

Founded as *La Villa Real de la Santa Fe de San Francisco de Assisi*, the natives try hard to keep that Spanish old-world atmosphere and the cultures of Indian, Mexican and early "Gringo" settlers. It celebrates many fiestas, which my family and I tried not to miss.

Among its many holidays is the annual De Vargas Procession, held in June on the two Sundays following Corpus Christi Sunday. The wooden statue of Our Lady of the Assumption —*La Conquistadora*— is carried from its chapel at St. Francis Cathedral through the streets to another sanctuary about a mile away.

In my readings of history, I learned that the statue was carved in Mexico and carried to Santa Fe by the Spanish conquistador Diego De Vargas as a symbol of the blessed virgin's patronage.

La Conquistadora was singled out for special honor during the 350th anniversary. Papal coronation was authorized by Pope John XXIII, and a crown was fashioned of precious metals and jewels funded from the donations of parishioners and townspeople. Another special tradition observed annually is called simply Fiesta. Tourist brochures say it is the oldest community celebration in the United States. Fiesta is held over the Labor Day weekend

A special place it is — in antiquity, in tradition, and in this wanderer's heart.

Nearly Famous Sayings

Horace Rumpole, esteemed defense lawyer of the Old Bailey courthouse in London, was as gruff and outspoken as he was witty. His creator was novelist John Mortimer, or *Sir John Mortimer* as the queen would have it. Mortimer wrote about Rumpole for the page and for a long-running television series. These are just a few of Rumpole's courtroom remarks:

The barrister once objected, spiritedly and daringly, to a judge's interruption in the courtroom proceedings. Rumpole correctly perceived that the judge was favoring the prosecution, as the judge had a reputation for doing. Turning to the jury, Rumpole declared while looking toward the bench and the bewigged judge, "Ladies and gentlemen of the jury, this is surely a case of premature adjudication."

-0-

Rumpole about opera: "There's an old saying that if it's something too silly to say, you can sing it."

-0-

On another occasion: "If I don't like the way the times are moving, I shall refuse to accompany them."

-0-

Shaking his fist, he shouted to his colleagues: "Cursed be those who steal this book."

-0-

In the tradition of Rumpole, actor Al Pacino said, in a movie eulogy for a gangster friend, "We die twice, once when our breath leaves our bodies and then when the last person we know quietly recalls our name."

JFK, Margarita & I

Jack and Jacqueline Kennedy. Mythical figures from their days of Camelot.

The first thing that comes to mind when I think back to that time is a presidential visit to Mexico in July, 1962. Unfortunately, my brain also brings back memories of a personal incident, an instant of regret almost too long ago to remember but one I will never forget.

I was a young reporter with The Associated Press in New York at the time, and one of several that were assigned to cover that JFK visit to Mexico City. While there, Jack and Jacqui were to attend a special mass at the centuries-old Nuestra Señora de Guadalupe shrine on a hill called Tepayac.

Their host was Mexican President Adolfo Lopez Mateos.

I was assigned to do a "color" story — a report on the crowded scene outside the Roman Catholic church, to include quotes of some of the nighborhood residents and the general goings of those curious well-wishers who had not been officially invited to attend. It would be a sidebar to the main story, which would come from reporters and photographers traveling with the President and Mrs. Kennedy.

The AP was relied on for the speed and accuracy of its reporting to member newpapers worldwide.

I was there at least two hours before the appointed time, walking and talking among the neighbors and some of those in the crowd already gathered there. I remember the residential area around the venerated church was old and some of it downright shabby. I wrote down notes and quotes and details.

When the presidential entourage arrived, the two presidents and their ladies left their limousines, flashed their smiles and waved to the cheering onlookers and disappeared inside. The Mass proceeded.

At the point where the Kennedys and their hosts were inside the basilica, I planned to drive back to our Mexico City bureau and write a detailed story that would be on our "wire services" as soon as possible. However, in our planning, we had failed to account for my getting through the massive crowds, the possibility of traffic tie-ups, numerous roadblocks by security officials and the like.

I soon realized it would take me hours to get downtown to the AP office, if I could find my car in the tumult.

What to do? Find a telephone and dictate a story. But where in that poor area of the 1960s? Impossible, until I thought of an elderly lady with whom I had chatted during the waiting hours. Margarita was friendly and reminded me of my grandmother. She was staying at home away from the crowds, she had told me, because she couldn't walk very far. Her dark eyes had widened at the masses of people and the strangeness of the situation in her usually quiet neighborhood.

I walked, trotted and then ran hard to get to her house. Hopefully, hopefully, she had a telephone and could help.

It turned out she was a lifesaver. Her house *did* have a working telephone. (I had tried two others along the way that didn't.) I sat panting in her tiny but tidy living room and dictated a longish story to our bureau. Afterward, she and I grinned at each other. I briefly hugged her as I thanked her profusely and hurried out of her small house.

But too quickly, it now seems these many years later.

I remember her to this day, her remaining teeth still fixed in a big smile but her pleading eyes seeming to ask for something else — the few pesos I should have offered, I realize now. Things happened so quickly, but I failed to repay a small kindness with one that would have been of much bigger value to her.

And I've regretted that ever since. I have her image engraved in my brain, and it won't go away whenever I think back to those long-ago days.

Older But Better

Hey, the wise and aging gentleman once said, not all of us get dumber as we get older.

Sensing more to come, I put on my thinking cap and ask him to explain. And he readily goes on:

I know Alheimers' sufferers get all the press, and we all understand and sympathize. My point is that in reality, a lot of us often get slower but *wiser* over the passing years.

Yes, we ache and complain, scurry to doctors and are in and out of emergency rooms and hospitals. But, often, in "our gathering years" — as a friend insists on saying — we put to use the accumulation of our thoughts and experiences.

Some of us have traveled to far-off places. Some are bursting with academic learning or scientific doing. We sometimes go off and experience different cultures and speak several languages besides our own. We volunteer, sometimes risking our lives in so doing.

In short, you name it. In 50, 60 and even 70 years beyond secondary schools and college, many old geezers and prissy old ladies are still active and doing. We write. We paint. Some of our clan tutor or take to classroom teaching. And some just sit and watch the tube or do housework or woodwork.

We're definitely slower, but not necessarily slow-witted. We don't use many modern gadgets and maybe we men don't shave as often as we should (but take a look at the younger 'personalities' on the television). We walk and talk and sometimes run and take the time to tell stories to our grandkids and enjoy nature (while it's still here).

And we shut up and listen to older and wiser heads, if there are any around.

In short, we run the gamut of doing, and often do it better than we used to.

Betrayals of the body can be dismaying. And carcinoma and G.I. problems are showing up with frequency. The vision blurs, and hearing is perhaps reduced. Tennis and golf may be off the list.

But, as writer Frank Bruni once put it, 'We have tricks of the mind and tools of the spirit infinitely more potent than the ravages of time.'

Seeing that I was nodding off, the friendly old gentleman veers off in a new direction. On the lighter side of things, he says, here's a joke that ahould illustrate something or other:

The rain was pouring and there was a big puddle in front of the pub. A ragged old man was standing there hanging a rod and string into the puddle. A tipsy, curious gentleman came over to him and asked what he was doing.

"Fishing," the old man said simply.

Poor old fool, the gentleman thought. So he invited the poor fool into the pub for a drink. As they were sipping, the young gentleman thought he should start some conversation. He asked the old man "And how many have you caught."

"You're the eighth," the old man replied.

Problems are just challenges to be overcome, my friend continues, just as we have overcome wars and economic depressions, and the false hopes and the many mistakes of our youth. We try to do positive things because we now have a lesser margin for error than we did in our youth.

Miami Cabbie

Years ago, a friend and I stepped into a Yellow Cab in Miami, where one became used to directing the driver in Spanish just to make sure he understood the English part. This rainy night in South Beach, we must have gotten the only cabbie who wasn't Latino.

And he didn't know much English, either.

I tried some more English and then Spanish again. No! French? No. Portuguese? No. He happpened to be Greek. He might as well have spoken Cantonese, Korean or Japanese, none of which I knew.

Eventually, with his pidgin English and my gesturing and urging, we made it to our destination, a short trip to Lincoln Road Mall.

As my companion and I were stepping out, I noticed a dictionary on the seat next to him. He shrugged, looked at me sheepishly and indicated that he was going to school in his spare time — to study Spanish!

Challenges

I've been doing it for so long, I don't know how to stop. I don't want to. It's always been a challenge for me, and I've always felt I needed to prove something to myself by doing it. The only difference now is that I'm completely free to do it when I get to it.

And because I don't make my living by doing it anymore, it's become pure pain as well as pleasure.

The challenge has always been to *write* in such a way as to attract readers. I used to have many. Now, I don't have so many. But I soon dispensed with the idea of attracting a wide readership, aiming instead to interest only myself, my family members and some of my friends.

The reason for all of this is that I used to write news stories, some call it journalism, for The Associated Press, which is known, respected and published worldwide. The other side of the coin is that after retirement (way after my AP retirement) I needed a new challenge and decided to write a book.

This often leads to a different way of thinking and may involve a radical change. An independent writer will have to approach the subject in a different way, think about it differently. He may have to conduct extensive research and spend months or years in tracking down people and esoteric details. Writing novels, nonfiction or poetry requires a great deal of patience. And I'm not even talking about getting a manuscript past a literary agent into the hands of an understanding editor at a publishing house. That's a different job all its own.

Some writers can make the transition easily. With others it takes time. I fell into the latter category.

Of course, I knew the readership would be much more limited for books than writing about news events, or even Sunday feature stories. A professional writer who has experienced the hard work, and gone through many of the trials and errors, may eventually acquire a huge readership. Along with that comes fame and money.

To some, writing comes easy. but I've never heard anyone say so. It's usually the other way around. Writers most often say the process is lengthy and tortuous. One may spend years writing a manuscript and, in the end, find no one willing to publish it — for many and varied reasons. I've experienced some of this.

I had written books before my retirement (the products were known as ghost books — for other people), so in my old age I thought I would try it again, but to do it for myself. Why not, what's there to lose, I thought, except for time and I thought I had plenty of that. I found out there is never enough of that. But I'm still doing it into my mid-80s.

Ohhhh, such a lonely, rocky road.

It's some of the hardest work I've ever done. In the past, I've written in and about strange and lonely foreign places, about catastrophic events, political skullduggery, spaceships, riots and people, important and otherwise. Those reports were usually under deadline, and some written under trying conditions.

Today, I write on what pleases me, about ideas I think should be expanded. I do it because I can't stop, as I say. I enjoy it — more-or-less, I think — because it's a challenge. The reward is to see your work in print. If I can interest a few readers, fine. If not, not. I'm not in it for money. I would starve if I were.

Perhaps to make this more understandable, and probably more interesting, I will tell you about my friend Bob and how he met his challenges. Lamentably, my friend Robert Lebrón, died in 2013. Bob was a master painter, an artist who once sold his classic, impressionist paintings for a great deal of money (sometimes as much as $15,000 to $20,000 for a painting).

Now, impressionists in general are not in great favor, unless you happen to have been Renoir or Monet or even Matisse or Lautrec. But Bob stuck to it. That's the kind of guy he was. That's what he did for as long as he cared to remember. And he took it very seriously.

He died in the summer of 2013.

He started doing his thing by carefully flattening out brown paper bags in his native lower Manhattan neighborhood and using them as his canvases, spread out on the sidewalk, to draw on. This was as a kid, some 75 years ago. Bob grew up a short, handsome man with thick dark hair that refused to turn gray. Even in his 60s and 70s, he thought of himself as a ladies' man.

With a little training and self-schooling, his native talents eventually expressed themselves in elegant street scenes of the skylines of Paris, Chicago, New York's Central Park, classic Western scenes and cowboys, and so many, many more. Perhaps you own one or have seen some of his paintings in a nice gallery somewhere in Palm Beach, Philadelphia, Miami or New York, or possibly New Hope, Pennsylvania.

He's illustrated some of my work: Painting a beautiful cover of two cowboys with the round, yellow ball of the moon as a background (this for *General Pancho and the Preacher*), and drawings on various topics for other books.

As I've indicated, the market for impressionist work continues to go downhill. But Bob, until his death, still got up every morning at 5:30 and worked steadily until 2 p.m. or so, painting and sketching. Occasionally, a gallery would sell one of his works at a good price, enabling him to keep going.

His life was a perfect illustration of what I'm trying to say: Some of us will continue to do our thing 'til our brains finally inform us what our bodies have been telling us for years: Stop. Enough. The End.

Tren de Muerte

Pues, si, íbamos, yo y mi compa,' caminando en la via del ferrocarril y sacando la garra.

A esa hora de la noche obscura sabiámos que siempre pasaba por alli, a cierta hora, un tren especial cargado con autos, cajas enormes, montones de hierros, y a veces, con vacas encerradas detras de barras de madera

El tren de la linea Santa Fe se llamaba "Rapid Zephyr," y, pues si, estaba llegando a la hora designada.

A nuestros oídos, se escuchaba bastante lejos, donde rodeaba una barranca. Choo, Choo. Choooo, Choo: Soplaba como chifle por los montes y las montañas obscuras y silenciosas.

Pues, nosotros seguiamos platicando y caminando sin problema porque sabíamos que a cierto punto el tren se desviaba, cruzandose por los rieles a otro rumbo. Rápido, rápido, el "Rapid Zephyr."

Pero, luego, *choo, chooo*, se oía bien cerca, interrumpiendo un poquito nuestros chistes, cuentos y mentiras.

Pues, si, ese tren nos tomó de sorpresa, por detrás, porque al punto mentado, el "Rapid Zephyr" no se desvio a ningun otro rumbo. Siguio directo. La noche era obscura, como digo, el tren muy agresivo, y nosotros muy preocupados. *Choo, Choo, ch-o-o-o-o.* Esa fue la ultima cosa que yo y mi compadre escuchamos en este mundo.

Choo, Choo, Choo, Choooo!

-0-

My friend and I were walking along the railroad tracks, joking, not looking. We knew a train was approaching, but we also knew that it would switch off onto another direction shortly before it reached us. Unfortunately, this dark night, the "Rapid Zephyr" for some reason did not transition over onto its second set of rails, and since we were laughing and not looking, the final sounds in life we heard, were Choo, choo, cho-o-o-o-o-o!

Solitude

In his murky way, Confuscius say: If you don't waste the time when you are alone, you will never be lonely.

Sometimes, fortune cookies carry excellent messages. Being Lonely, Solitude. aloness . . . Slighty different meanings. But some of our best creative writers have used them to their best advantage.

Taking a glance at the lives of a few of the best creative writers — D.H. Lawrence, James Joyce, Tolstoy, Dostoyevsky, Steinbeck, Ernie Pyle, Walter Mosley, Garcia Marquez, Emily Dickenson, Flannery O'Connor, Walt Whitman, Edgar Allen Poe, Carl Sandburg and so many others —you can see how, and why, much of their creative output came out of just sitting by themselves, thinking, maybe brooding. And then writing

Some of the best ones store up their experiences until they find their own lonely spot where they can write uninterrupted as long as they want.

Others take meticulous notes for anything they can work into a story later. Notes on quotes and characters and ideas can often be found strewn around the house.

Some writers, such as Hemingway, Steinbeck and Garcia Marquez would take long breaks away from their work. But they would come back and wait until they found their moods, or until they could compose their brains and notes around what they wanted to say. Poe, Flannery O'Connor, Dickenson and others often locked themselves away until they were satisfied with their work.

Here's something else:

You're in bed, turn off the light and can't go to sleep. You can't get your brain to stop working. You start to remember stuff you thought you had forgotten. It may be that you embroider the past, turn fact into fiction or the other way around. You may argue with yourself. I should have done this in my life. Or, I'm ashamed for doing that. You wander around in your brain and pick and choose what you want out of it.

You might jump out of bed and look for a pencil and paper. You write.

It's a good thing to do. It cleanses the soul. You are creating something out of solitude and sleeplessness. And, who knows, it may turn into a bestseller.

Music

My life would have been incomplete without heavy doses of music.

I'm no musician — unless you count the triangle in grade school and the later banging on drums — but I am an attentive, knowledgeable listener. a self-described student of some of the history of jazz and the classics. Music has always been emotional and enchanting for me. I get lost in it. It envelops my brain and very soul.

I envy those talented men and women who can produce the sounds that move me. It's always surprising to me how ordinary and "just-folks" the musicians turn out to be once they are away from their magical powers up on the stage. Up there, in the lights, they are giants. But out in the crowd, they are ordinary people.

"It's not the money," a noted saxophonist explained to me while urinating at a half-stall next to mine during the intermission of a jazz concert. "I learned to play in grade school, then started performing with a band and liked the atmosphere and the crowds, or just the few drinkers who happened to be there — it didn't much matter, you know. I just kept learning the instrument, and I think now if I wasn't being paid to be doing this, I would somehow get up the money to pay them to be allowed to perform."

After zipping up and washing his hands, he turned at the door and added, "I'm glad to play for people who appreciate the music." He winked at me and hurried back to the main stage, the only thing that counted for him.

I have been blessed throughout the years with choices of venues — from some of the most renowned concert stages to the dingiest barroom dancehalls that dot the rural, dusty roads of this and several countries I can name. Wherever I ended up, it was a magical night for me. Virtually everything I chose was an exhilarating experience and often an emotional one as well.

Through various genres and individual musicians. I tried to choose what would please my ears, my brain, my heart and soul. I think I managed to do that most of the time. Except for bluegrass twanging and being bitten my dozens of mosquitoes at an outdoor concert in Tallahassee, I enjoy almost anything. But there are other exceptions, such as rap. I won't even start on that subject.

In my early days, at home and in the military in the 1940s and '50s, the radio widened my world by bringing me the sounds of George Shearing, Dave Brubeck, and the big bands such as those of Stan Kenton, Bill Basie, Ellington and magnificent performers such as Billy Butterfield and Sarah Vaughn, Nat King Cole and Benny Goodman among them. I never expected that I would later have opportunities to see and experience the sounds of many of these musical geniuses in person.

Not only the music, but some of the venues have had their attractions. Carnegie Hall and Radio City Music Hall are unforgettable. I'm sorry to say, I never visited the Cotton Club in Harlem.

From the tinkly pianos, brassy horns and steady drumbeats emanating from New Orleans, Kansas City, Motown (Detroit and Memphis) New York and Chicago, L.A. and San Francisco and many of the places in-between, to the big bands and studio wax discs, the 78s,

45s, 33s, CDs, DVDs and computer streaming — jazz was always king for me.

I remember particularly well standing at the bar and watching Peggy Lee sing at Basin Street East in Manhattan. Then came Lionel Hampton at the Metropole, Miles Davis at Birdland and the small groups in Greenwich Village — Bill Evans at the Village Vanguard. plus the many I can't remember at the Village Gate, the Blue Note and Arthur's.

I was fortunate to see and hear Frank Sinatra in the 1950s while I was a student at the University of New Mexico in Albuquerque, and somewhere along the line Brubeck and his quartet (Brubeck, Paul Desmond, Joe Morello and Eugene Wright) added to my deep appreciation and education.

Later, the 1982 opening ceremonies of Walt Disney's EPCOT in Florida offered us an extravaganza of big bands — Basie, Glenn Miller, Hampton, Bob Crosby, Pete Fountain and others. Also making big music there was the West Point Glee Club. Wow. That's when the Walt Disney parks really excelled at throwing a party.

And, then, of course, there are the Mozarts and Verdis, Rachmaninoff, Beethoven and Debussy and so many others that came and left us their grand compositions that will last forever. I bow to the classics because they gave birth to much of what we listen to today.

The before-and after explications of the progress of classic jazz I will leave to others. But for me, everything else grew from that.

Jazz arrived decades ago to a lonely boy, trying to soften the hard days of his Depression-era life. Classical Music, ballet and a few operas were later refinements in musical education to me. I believe all music lovers are beholden to those centuries-old symphonies and their famous composers from which modern-day music emanated.

A favorite author Dennis Lehane puts it this way: "Music speaks for the soul because words are so small."

They

They were penniless when he and his love married, but they paid this no heed. Work hard, keep going, something good will come. They believed that. And, with little choice, that was the credo they followed. It worked out well enough all the way through.

There was always risk-taking in their life together, but they kept busy doing instead of just dreaming, although there was plenty of dreaming. And struggle. They always had that. But whoever said that life was easy?

To paraphrase Henry James, they tried to be among "those people on whom nothing in life was lost."

Ah, but not to forget the many changes along the way: From FDR through the Great Depression and the too-many wars, then JFK, LBJ, MLK and up to the moon and back. Then there was a president who was black, who made this nation proud of itself and the grandeur of its history.

To have been a part of this process in one lifetime — and to have been privileged to live it, and for him to write about small parts of it — is too sweet even to have dreamed about.

In those days of the mid-20th Century, and long before, those who found themselves in straitened circumstances didn't depend on the government, the taxpayer, to make right any of their own stupid errors. They labored to get themselves out of tough situations or . . . they didn't! Period. Those who endured know what that's all about.

It has become an entirely different world, of course. "Responsibility" has lost its meaning.

They savored the precious time together as family, and each was forever humbled by the sacrifices made by the other, and those around them. Looking back, it was daunting to see the many obstacles overcome, some that came as crushing, unexpected blows.

One thing he and she learned for sure, just as Carl Sandburg once wrote, it *is* possible to conquer sorrow. They mainly recalled the joys of life and few of the sorrows, and there were both a-plenty. Somehow, in failing memory, the best seemed to always win out over the worst.

The Tourist

Jaime was an American citizen who had lived in this country for more than two decades, but he always wanted to go back to his native Cuba. "For a visit only," he hastened to say. "I love the U.S. but I can't resist the nostalgia, the lure of my Cuban homeland."

Like some, we may not even like our hometown, but we always want to go back there — to see what it's like, find out if any of the old gang is still around, just experience the place once again. If we want, we can even call up the special times and even the smells, which lurk there in the back of our brains.

The place where we were born and grew up in always summons us back. That is our *real* first love. Jimmy, everybody calls him that — you know how it is with Americans — Jimmy got his chance to go back, for a short visit.

El Regreso the return. That had been his longtime goal. Nothing political.

He saw an opportunity and he took it. Strangely, that chance came through a fishing trip, of all things, since he didn't fish. But, hey, why turn down Providence.

You must understand, we're talking about a time of personal danger in Communist Cuba for just about everybody. Americans may not have known it, but in the 1970s and even into the '80s, foreigners were still under suspicion, even as invited "guests." Hotel rooms were bugged, particularly in Havana (government-controlled desk clerks assigned the rooms). Restaurants, nightclubs, tourist sites were closely watched for suspicious activities by anyone, everyone.

The G2 was lurking even though the Cuban dictatorship of Fidel Castro wanted foreign exchange, preferably greenbacks. It wasn't the turbulent 1960's but it wasn't that distant from it in many ways.

Officially, there had been no diplomatic relations between the United States and Cuba since the Bay of Pigs invasion in April, 1961. The U.S. prohibited travel to Cuba for Americans except for journalists, academicians, and specially invited groups which stayed together and were escorted everywhere as one. Routinely, Cubans suspected that many Americans were spies, anyway. And if someone strayed away from his assigned group, he might be in for big trouble.

Getting back to Jimmy. He had a couple of American friends who were big-time bass fishermen. None of that interested Jimmy. His friends gave him the idea to join up with a newly organized tour.

At the time, there was an American company that *contracted* with the Cuban government to take Americans to the island from Florida on fishing excursions. The company was said to be the first U.S. firm to sign a commercial pact with the Cuban dictatorship since Fidel Castro came to power in 1959.

Company officials assured everyone signing up that they would be perfectly safe. "We've never lost anybody," the owner used to say.

Jimmy paid his $695 and signed up with Cuba Tours USA, Inc.

The St. Petersburg-Clearwater airport served as the takeoff point. They were to try their luck at Lago del

Tesoro, Treasure Lake, which was true to its name. Think of it, a lake full of bass, landlocked tarpon and other excellent fighting fish — and few fishermen. A paradise!

Treasure Lake was deep in the Zapata Swamp about 100 miles southeast of Havana. The treasure was in its 8- and 10-pound black bass. The true fishermen were all dreaming of a world-record catch. Besides, there were the silver king *Sabalo*, or tarpon, which were in the lake before anything else.

The group was bused into the interior from Havana the next day and everyone was registered into a little village "camp" called Guama, a former Indian village now duded out for tourists. It was on the shore of Lago Tesoro and had all the amenities Americans could want — restaurant, two bars, swimming pool, dance floor.

Even Jimmy went out on the fabled lake, with his friends from New Jersey. He was supplied with fishing tackle and had his hook baited with the proper lure. The fish were so plentiful, this complete novice hooked onto a big one that hot first afternoon, but he failed to "set" the hook and the fish — maybe a trophy-sized bass, the others said — wiggled away and disappeared.

As the days went by, though, Jimmy became anxious. He had come to see and experience his homeland. So, what am I doing here, he asked himself. In this sham of a Taino Indian village? He was unhappy with what the Castro regime had allowed its cash-paying *gringos* to do.

He made a fateful decision, daring to set out on his own.

So in the dark and stillness of the following morning, only the jungle rustlings and the buzz of mosquitoes accompanied him as he made his way to a prearranged spot near the campground where he was picked up by the driver of an old, rattling truck which had just delivered the daily supplies to Guama.

The truck, along with Jaime, was returning to Santiago.

Jaime's thinking was, the Castro G2 is not concerned with a nobody. Why should they bother about me if I take off from this place? I have a right to get another look at the home of my ancestors, this Cuban-American thought. They don't *own* this country.

His grandma, who raised him, was long dead, but he had distant relatives in that southeast region of Cuba. He was born in Santiago de Cuba, not far from Guama, and his family lived in Santiago many years. His father attended schools there, had gone on to the university and become a respected physician before having to escape into exile with his life.

As they rattled along the winding, narrow road, Jaime's only thoughts were of his family and two friends, his boyhood playmates, whom he thought of as brothers. Ramon and Miguel had stayed behind. And he hadn't heard a word from them, or about them, since the invasion at Bahia de Cochinos, the Bay of Pigs, in 1961.

Many a Cuban, friend and foe, had been killed during that ill-fated operation. It had forever changed that island nation. Like the American Civil War, it had broken up families, setting brother against brother, in some cases, and affecting many others indirectly.

What had been his "brothers'" fate?

The truck arrived on the outskirts of Santiago before daybreak. Saying a quick goodbye, Jaime embraced the driver, Jose, and his son Arturo, who were risking their delivery business, if not their freedom, in helping him. Jaime gave them many pesos and set out on his own. "Vaya con Dios," Jose called out.

Jaime went looking for his brothers.

He was quickly reunited with several members of his family and saw a few friends from his schooldays. The second day of his furtive visit, Jaime ran into an old friend named Raul, who was drinking a beer and chatting with friends at the neighborhood bar.

"Hijo, pero eres tu?" Is that really you, Raul asked in surprise.

The two embraced heartily. They had been in high school together, but Raul also had remained behind with his family and was now a supervisor at a sugar refinery.

"Mira, Raul, I really shouldn't be here," Jaime told him. And he told him the details of his trip. "Anyway, I just want to look up Ramon and Miguelito, you remember them, *mis hermanos*. We were inseparable."

Raul looked around and kept ignoring his question. "You look good, amigo."

"I've always wanted to come back, Raul. And now I'm here. And before I leave this country again, I want to see them. I haven't heard a word since my father, mother, sister and I sneaked away in the middle of the night to go into *exilio*. That was a long time ago. We were children."

Raul finally took Jaime into a dark corner and quietly said, *"Ellos son rebeldes."* They became rebels against Castro.

Jaime was not too surprised. *"Donde?"* he asked. Where?

"Pues, en la capital y por allá." In Havana and around there, Raul whispered, moving Jaime farther away from his drinking friends.

Raul haltingly told him of some places to ask about his brothers, but he had urged caution "because the Castro people can track you down and make you disappear forever into La Cabaña prison." Raul then wanted to hear no more of Jaime's plans. It was dangerous for him and his family to even have contact like this.

Jaime left Santiago, boarding a chugging *guagua,* a rattletrap bus that took all day to get to Havana. At least, Jaime now knew what had become of his brothers: They had rebelled against the Castro regime. They must be in hiding and striking out against the government whenever they saw an opportunity. He was told there were small rebel groups throughout the island.

Maybe it was lucky for Jaime that when he arrived in Havana, everyone's attention seemed to be focused on an international fishing event: the Ernest Hemingway Memorial Billfish Tournament. It was the first time in some twenty years that American boaters were permitted to take part in the annual competition named for the famous author who once lived and wrote in Cuba.

Needing the dollars, Cuba's National Institute for Tourism was opening up the gates to free-spending Yankee skippers and their crews once again.

So Jaime mingled freely, and kept his ears open. He didn't expect any major acts of rebellion during the big event, but he was hoping to get enough clues to put two-and-two together about his brothers' whereabouts.

Along the way, gregarious Cuban fishermen who enthusiastically joined the tournament *turistas* were talkative. They liked this Cuban-American who talked to them in their language. Jaime put all of his tidbits of information together the next day and came up with some good clues about the rebels and their haunts.

One place to go for more information on the rebels, he determined, was a waterfront bar in the Old Havana suburb of Regla, which was just across the bay from the teeming over-populated capital. This was definitely a working-class hangout, whose barmaids served the cheapest Bacardí and Ironbeer. At the cafe, all questions were referred to a short, beefy cigar-smoking overseer with heavy-lidded eyes and coal black hair, who sat at a table in the shadowy gloom with several friends.

Jaime's English-tinged Spanish and his clothes had quickly marked him to Señor Franco as a Cuban-American. Franco tried to limit his disdain for this visitor, whom he had seen on earlier visits to the bar, but he saw some quick money could be had.

"Señor Franco, I don't care about the chicken and black beans," Jaime immediately launched into his prepared remarks. "I've been informed, with some authority, that you have knowledge of some of the rebels in this country. I am looking for my brothers, and I would like your help."

Franco blinked and straightened in his chair in astonishment. The others at the table moved quickly away.

"If what you have been told would happen to be true, what makes you think I would tell you anything," Franco replied, drawing out the words.

"Señor Franco, you can check up on me, if you want. I am, in a way, a desperate man, probably sought by the police right now. I want to find my boyhood friends,

Ramon and Miguel, and see if I can help them in some way before I go back to the States.

"Get out of here," growled Franco abruptly.

Meeting over. No information, no threats, *nada*.

Outside the bar, though, Jaime encountered a scrawny, bearded man who had been sitting at the table with Franco.

"What makes you think your friends are rebellious to the authorities in our present government?" the skinny, bearded one asked.

Jaime spent a half hour in another bar with the nondescript bearded man, whose name he never learned. At the end, he was told he would be contacted soon. That was that. Jaime went away bewildered, convinced that he had been stupid and foolhardy; that he had probably put his friends at greater risk.

The G2 will probably be knocking on my door at 2 a.m., he thought.

It didn't take that long for results, however. At nightfall, while walking through a small park in the square facing his hotel, Jaime was approached by another bearded man and given an address. "Be there tonight at 11," the man said. And he was gone.

The address was deep in the backstreets of the Havana harbor, and by *guagua*, a taxi ride and a lot of walking down dark streets, he finally got to his destination: Apartmento 9 in a rundown building on a dead-end street called Calle Bullosa.

He knocked tentatively, and the door was immediately thrown open by a tall, stocky, fully bearded man.

"Jaime," the man said emotionally, hugging him, while at the same time patting him down quickly. "I am Miguel."

"*Miguel, sí. Mi hermano! Estás bien?*"

"I am well," Miguel said, sitting him down at a small table. "*Y tu? Como va el exilio?*"

"Exile has worked out well, Miguel. I've come to look for you and Ramon and to offer you my help. Where is he?"

"Ramon was killed about a year ago," Miguel said, relaxing, taking his time now, telling him about an attack against a military base not far from Matanzas. The *militares* shot dead three of his small rebel group. But the rebels escaped with weapons and grenades. Among those left behind was Ramon, however.

"What are you doing here?" Miguel asked Jaime. "It is dangerous for you to be with me."

"Miguel, I know what you are doing. I want to be with you, become one of you."

"You cannot do that," Miguel replied. "It is too late for any help anymore. We are small in number and getting smaller. It will end soon, one way or another."

Jaime started to protest when there was a small explosion on the street outside, followed by a huge blast that knocked them to the floor and sent rubble crushing down upon them. Men in uniform quickly followed, spraying the room and its occupants with automatic weapons.

"*Ya terminó todo para estos cabrones,*" the leader of the invading unit shouted at his men. "Stop shooting. These sons of bitches are done for. Move on."

Although Jaime, Miguel, Ramon and others like them have disappeared from the scene, and the Castro *revolucion* has moved on, so have the anti-Castro rebels. They have not disappeared and continue to fight their small battles, watching and waiting — through these many, many long years in the history of Cuba.

Grenada War

It may seem strange to say at this time, but I have never known such peace and tranquility as I did on a beautiful Sunday evening in a battle-scarred little town named for Saint George.

The townfolk were using an imposing 18th Century church on this occasion to memorialize those killed in a brief battle with invaders during the short-lived Grenada War. The invaders to this volcano-created island were U.S. Marines and Army troops who had suffered a few of their own casualties, along with Cuban soldiers and civilians.

The Cubans were busy building an airport in St. George's and President Ronald Reagan feared the hilly island was becoming "a Soviet-Cuban colony being readied as a major military bastion to export terror and undermine democracy." Another reason given for the invasion — later mocked as Reagan's Little War — was to protect American students at a medical school in Grenada.

It's all in the history books.

The church preacher gave a heartfelt sermon at that overflowing church in the services held just before nightfall. Emotional speeches and colorful ceremonies followed. There were tearful, spontaneous eulogies by some of the relatives of those who had been killed. The wounded and imprisoned were recognized. Other congregants paid eloquent tribute to all of the battle's casualties — Americans, Cubans and Grenadians.

And then there was singing.

The individual, melodic voices of talented church members who knew those hymns by heart stood out from others of the colorfully dressed church-choir members, but all was sung in such a synchronized manner that any other time might have taken weeks of practice. I stood in awe, and reflected on my own life as I'm sure others in attendance did.

With the only light coming from the wide-open windows, those elegant psalms echoed throughout that ancient building in a way that moved us all. Everyone held hands and joined in. Even strangers were offered hymnals and urged to sing along. I'm sure that wonderful singing rang throughout the terraced streets of that entire town and even into the forested countryside. I sometimes still hear it in my mind.

When it was over, we were all left speechless and wondering at the ruthless nature of men at war, who fight each other over political ideologies that may mean little in the long run — especially to those who try to live their quiet lives in peace among their neighbors.

The warriors and politicians would continue to have their way throughout the world, but it would all have different meaning to those most directly affected. This was was the case with those bewildered, hard-working residents of St. George's now coming together in such prideful sadness.

Just Saying

A passing thought or two.

The United States of America became as imperialistic as its mother country for many years, there is no denying that. It continued along those lines for too long, adding to its huge territory by crafty bargaining and warfare, if need be.

Over its short history, my country has become a world power as much for its vastness and wealth in physical resources as for its military. Along witth that, much of its fiscal power has been available to friends, and even several foes, in foreign lands. It contributes a great deal of its knowledge and culture to the world.

It has participated in great wars largely, but not always, on principle.

It continues as the world ideal of a great democracy, which includes many of democracy's failings. Its technology and its human brainpower has been unmatched until recently, when the rest of the world inevitably catches up and sometimes surpasses in some fields.

This grand young nation has had its share of dirty dealings along with its goodnesses.

And, like all countries in this world, faces many challenges.

I applaud valid criticism but protest the rantings of those who set themselves up as ultimate authorities and loudly proclaim that everything is terrible in this North American country between Mexico and Canada.

One example of this are the writings of the late Chilean poet Pablo Neruda, who won the Nobel Prize in Poetry primarily by proclaiming the "evil" that he found in the United States while praising the glories of Fidel Castro and other despots of the Americas, Europe and Africa.

Particularly repugnant are his poetry and patter in praise of his hero, the rebel comandante Castro, who plunged that Caribbean nation into its worst economic and cultural depression in its history. But, then, the Nobel laureate was highly regarded by some American academicians for his maddened bluster and even invited to lecture in this den of evil. They bid desperately to acquire the rights to his papers after his death.

Contrast an open democracy with the closed societies in which Neruda and the Castro Cubans lived in for innumerable years.

But why bother with trivialities, one might say. They are too unimportant now, as our planet, the only home we have, approaches its own self-created end through its own neglect.

Should not that be the focus of our democratic comittment?

French Fries

There's got to be a lesson in here somewhere.

When my youngest granddaughter was a little more than 2 years old, she would sometimes get it in her head that if she cried and wailed long enough she might get what she wanted *right now*.

One day, we were all in the car — my other granddaughter beside me in the passenger seat, her parents in back with their daughter Lexi between them. We were in somewhat of a hurry to get to a store before it closed (yes, grocery stores used to close down for the night). Suddenly, Lexi decides now would be a good time to cry and carry on about something she's just got to have.

Her mother's admonishments failed to shut her up. Her father could do no better. So I spoke out gruffly from the driver's seat. Looking directly at her in the rearview mirror, I said, "Lexi, what do you want? Say it again slowly and quit yelling." Her big, beautiful dark eyes widened, and all of a sudden she couldn't think of anything to say. She fidgeted but quieted and looked out the window. She didn't let out another peep.

We got to the store in time, did our shopping and as we were walking out the door, my granddaughter left her mother's grasp and slipped in beside me. She grabbed my hand and held it. Looking up, she said, "Grandpa."

"Yes."

"Can we get French Fries?" (she called them fench fies).

Of course the first thing we did on the way home was to stop in at the local MacDonald's and get her some French Fries, and ice cream for everybody. Lexi had seen the big, yellow street sign on the way out: That big yellow M — a magnet for children of all ages.

Child Education

Here's the wise old man again, sittin' and a-rockin' employing his philosophy upon his two guests, who enjoy listening to his words of wisdom:

"You know, all this talk about poorly performing students and ill-prepared teachers? Well, hardly ever do any of those double-domed experts talk about the students' parents. To me, these kids' parents are the ones who should be held responsible, along with any classroom faults," the old man starts off.

"Schoolchildren are not doing their work and hardly disciplined, and educators are not adequately prepared, they say. Well, a lot of it boils down to those moms and dads who send them off with a sandwich and a dollar. Some don't even do that. They want the schools to feed them, too.

"Many parents are too busy to bother with their children. A kid to them is like a kitchen appliance, to be treated like a toaster or a fancy fridge.

"They devote more time to their TV-watching and their smart phones than they do to their children," he continued. "You notice that most of those poor people featured on the tv have 50-inch screens, gold jewelry, smart phones and fancy watches. How do they pay for all of this if they're so poor? They're the ones most often complaining that they don't get any help from the feds, which means the rest of us.

"So along come these 'experts' and tell us all what's wrong in the classroom. And they come up with these fancy solutions to the problems. But hardly do I see them write or talk about *why* these kids are so," the wise old man said.

"I'll tell 'em why. By the time a child goes to school, it may be too late to try to teach him or her anything. The time to begin teaching the little one is the day after he or she is born. The ideas of right and wrong should not be ignored during these growin' up years. And discipline and manners should follow right along.

"And that's what I think about a child's education. How about you?"

Havana Night

It was a cold summer night in Havana.

The wind was blowing leaves and tree branches at what seemed like 50 mph. Dark gray clouds appeared and quickly scooted away, suddenly there and suddenly gone. The hot day had turned into a shivery evening. We had enjoyed the beautiful beach and hot sun at nearby Varadero earlier that day.

I looked out at the balcony area and could see that windy gusts had cleared it of everything but two metal chairs and a table, surprisingly still holding two glasses. We were in the middle of a sudden storm that was to become a hurricane.

The scene was my top-floor apartment in a four-story building at the corner of Veintiuna and O, across the street from the famous Hotel Nacional.

The whining wind soon brought flapping sheets of rain. Through the windows, I could vaguely discern monster waves crashing over the rockface walls braced against the sea. Ocean water flowed up, down and through Malecon Boulevard, collecting debris as it went and piling it into bordering greenery.

The Atlantic must have been roiling dark, I shuddered to think.

Just a few minutes earlier, my companion and I had been enjoying a leisurely drink on that patio balcony, our eyes fixed on a beautiful sunset struggling to glow through raven clouds. Soon, those clouds ominously darkened further, growing and shifting our way. We hurried inside, and I closed the sliding-glass balcony door to the living room.

Eventually, we went to bed knowing that the storm would blow over that part of northern Cuba during the night. It had happened before and it would happen again. We might be at the tail-end of another hurricane. The radio had made no mention of that possibility.

We were too-soon awakened by rumbling and rattling sounds. "What's that," she said, sitting straight up in bed. It was raining, I knew. And the wind was groaning. But the sounds we heard were more than all that.

Suddenly, she and I could feel a rush of cold air coursing the length of the house. It raced through the living room and the dining and kitchen areas, and it was now reaching sideways like crab claws into the bedroom.

"It's that glass door at the balcony," I yelled back after jumping up and moving fast.

In the hallway, through dim lamplight, I saw the balcony door, all eight feet of it, swinging backward out of its bottom track toward the living room. It would then go crashing forward out toward the balcony. The six-foot sheet of glass was holding inside its metal frames, but the entire door was wildly swinging with each wind-and-rain gust.

My lady friend and I struggled and strained getting the door back on its track, not sure it wouldn't come crashing down on us. But I knew those efforts alone wouldn't hold the door in its place. I was fearful, too, that it would suddenly go crashing onto the balcony and the street below.

So I grabbed several boards I had planned to use in building a spare table. Luckily, a hammer and nails were nearby, too. Without much thinking, I criss-crossed two of the lengthier boards over the balcony door and nailed them into the wall facings. We hurriedly positioned black tape against the boards and the other windows facing the sea.

That held everything together, although it was a sad sight to see. Sleep for the night went out that window, so to speak. But I never forgot that lesson. Always keep boards, nails and strong tape handy for the next strong blow that knocks on the door.

Something to Say

He had something to say and little time to say it, so he wrote it down, and here it is.

He led a scattershot kind of life, never really focusing on any *one* thing. He wanted to make that clear at the outset. It's what really formed him. Not focusing was both good and bad. He was into everything, and nothing in particular. That was not considered a bad thing in his youth. A liberal education, in-and-out of school, with a glimpse into the arts, was good.

Soon enough — after the military and during his time at university — he haphazardly landed in journalism, which was then objective reporting and writing. And he then did that in one form or another all the way through life. He hadn't planned it that way, but he was glad it happened.

In effect, his rough education in life's humanities, as it were, helped him understand people and the value of keeping-on with learning. It showed him that his way in that world was about asking the right questions and often determining that not all the answers were what they seemed.

Learning turned out to be a lifetime immersion: into experience, reading, writing, music learning and listening, and family life, photography, challenges of all sorts. He had a special facility for the daily give-and-take with other cultures and with people who led far different lives than his. He knew and loved several "foreign" languages and the origin of certain words.

Some of his most satisfactory journalism dealt with people and their often-difficult daily lives in what were then distant places — among them, Cuba, Portugal, Spain, Grenada, Barbados, Haiti, the Dominican Republic, Trinidad and the other Caribbean islands, and The Bahamas and, later, Brazil.

To learn about people, he often lived among them: He ate rice and beans in the mountains of southeast Cuba with Fidel's friends. He drank *cafezinhos* and harsh *cachaza* with cattle barons in Brazil's Rio Grande do Sul, and he gladly shared the Portuguese fishermen's *bacalhau* after spending a day with them on the water. He remembers the Sunday bullfights in and around Madrid, celebrating with the crowds when the matador received a bull's bloody ear or tail.

Everywhere he went, he drank the good, and not-so-good wine and the local rum. He smoked the cigars, and he stayed alongside as long as he could. He wrote about them, about what they believed in, what they and their wives and children did and dreamed about, weaving it all into the bigger events of the time.

But, precisely because some of these journalistic reports were "people stories" — not about their leaders' resounding rhetoric — some encountered problems of newspaper space back home. Editors then devoted much of their interest to the explosive news out of Moscow, Saigon, Washington and other Cold War hotspots of the time.

Vox pop often went by the wayside.

Alas. to this day — in what remains of the American newspaper — editors, and therefore readers, show little interest in different cultures and their history, not to mention the hopes and dreams of the people enveloped in those events. There are exceptions to this in excellent reports that go beyond our borders. Lamentably, not enough. Television sometimes brings the world closer.

Of course, sharing a pizza with *revolucionario* Fidel Castro, drinking Bloody Marys with writer Truman Capote and reporting on the courtroom hijinks of killer Ted Bundy were also a part of the overall picture this writer painted. Those immense personalities were the attraction.

After moving away from journalism and his "professional life," he achieved freedom in fiction and poetry.

Harking back to the words of Winston Groom, the author of Forrest Gump and other novels, "There was a loneliness and uncertainty and craziness that went along with a writer's life." Groom was talking specifically about novelists, but it applied to all of those who searched beyond the superficialities of life.

One of this writer's favorite authors, John Updike, once described his favorite protagonist as one "whose essential identity is a solitary one — to be found in flight and loneliness and even adversity." Updike went on to say that this seemed to him his "feeling of what being a human being involves."

His own thinking went along those same lines.

In sum, he believed that every encounter he ever had — with the famous, infamous and ordinary citizen — was an education to be then used, or stored for the proper time. He kept busy learning, taking something away from everything he witnessed or participated in, even many of the wrong things.

When people really learn, they adapt. And learn is the key word here. For instance, he learned he was once intolerant of many things. Later, he became a pushover for most. Old age allows one to learn from youth's mistakes, as someone sagely summed it up.

For him, the key to living peacefully in his own mind was to keep learning about himself and others — about who that other person is, what he does, where he fits in. He found he didn't have to be another Shakespeare, Sandburg or Gershwin, just an individual who got the most out of every day, just as Winston Groom's lonely, uncertain and crazy writers had. He was proud of that.

To paraphrase Carl Sandburg: There was joy on his face when he lived, and he hoped it would be there when he died.

Vatican Bibles

On a tour of the Vatican toward the end of a long day of photography not many years ago, I tired of the many crowded points of interest in those long corridors and dedicated chapels within that vast basilica.

There were stained glass windows, marble statues and famous paintings all around that I had duly depicted with various lenses under different lighting conditions, and I believed I had just about covered everything I possibly could.

I whispered to my friend that I was heading back toward the front and would meet him somewhere around the entrance. Walking away from the crowds and the waves of approaching sightseers, I finally managed to find myself virtually alone, trudging freely towards the emerging daylight of the vast entrance doors.

On my way, I noticed a deserted, darkened hallway off to my right just before I walked out. No guards, no signs, nothing to indicate that the various rooms on either side of that short passageway were occupied. The doors were closed, and no lights shone underneath. So my curiosity took hold and I decided to open one of the doors to take a look within.

The good-sized room was empty, except for a somewhat broken wooden chair leaning against a wall in a far corner. It held several stacks of books. The chair, which apparently had once been covered in white velvet, was next to a fullsize window looking out on a courtyard.

Sunshine streamed through fraying yellow-and-white silk curtains onto the chair holding the books.

Perfect lighting for a still picture, I thought. This little sidetrack might not have been fruitless after all.

I took the bold step of walking into the room, not thinking about what could happen to a Vatican City visitor in an unauthorized location. The closer I walked, the clearer the book bindings became. The books were aged and some were tattered, I noticed. When I got up to the chair I could see they were bibles, old bibles of various sizes, heaped there without much concern.

But the picture of those leather- and cloth-bound volumes piled on two stacks on that chair with the daylight streaming through fraying curtains was too good to pass up. I took a few steps back and photographed the scene. I then quickly moved out of there and found my friend by the entrance. We walked away, caught a taxi and went back to our hotel: two aging camera bugs happy as clams with their treasure trove of the day's adventures captured on digital disks.

Today, a 14x17-inch copy of that photograph hangs on a chapel wall in a large hospital in the Orlando area, with the simple caption, "Vatican Bibles."

Printed in the United States
By Bookmasters